Holiness:
Is It Attainable Today?

Monk Moses of Mount Athos

HOLINESS

IS IT ATTAINABLE TODAY?

Translated by
Fr. Peter A. Chamberas

HOLY CROSS ORTHODOX PRESS
Brookline, Massachusetts

© 2012 Holy Cross Orthodox Press

Published by Holy Cross Orthodox Press
50 Goddard Avenue
Brookline, Massachusetts 02445

ISBN 978-1-935317-33-3

Originally published in Greek as *I aghiotita einai katorthoti simera?*, vol. 14 of the series Athonika anthi [Athonite Flowers], Ekdoseis Tenos, Athens, 2010.

All rights reserved. No part of this publication may be reproduced, stored in a retrieval system, or transmitted in any form or by any means—electronic, mechanical, photocopy, recording, or any other—without the prior written permission of the publisher. The only exception is brief quotations in printed reviews.

Library of Congress Cataloging-in-Publication Data
Moses, Monk.
 [Aghiotita einai katorthoti simera? English]
 Holiness : is it attainable today? / Monk Moses of Mount Athos.
   p. cm. -- (Athonite flowers ; 14)
 ISBN 978-1-935317-33-3 -- ISBN 1-935317-33-4
 1. Holiness. 2. Christian saints. 3. Orthodox Eastern Church-- Doctrines. I. Chamberas, Peter A. II. Title.
 BT767.M6913 2012
 234'.8--dc23
                                                          2012006333

Contents

Translator's Foreword   vii
    Fr. Peter A. Chamberas

Foreword   ix
    Protopresbyter Athanasios Lagouros

1. With All the Saints   1

2. Holiness and the Saints   17

3. Fools for Christ   37

4. The New Martyrs of Chios   55

5. The All-Holy Theotokos   65

6. The Most-Compassionate Father   85

Translator's Foreword

Twelve years ago Holy Cross Orthodox Press introduced Elder Monk Moses of Mount Athos to the English-speaking world by publishing an anthology of seven essays on the spiritual life, essays selected from his early publications in the Greek series entitled Ἀθωνικὰ Ἄνθη ("Athonite Flowers"). Since then Fr. Moses has continued to write most insightfully and beautifully on the many aspects of the spiritual tradition in the Orthodox Church.

The Athonite Flowers series, which is very popular throughout Greece, has now reached fourteen volumes. It is this latest volume of Athonite Flowers, published by Tenos Publications in Athens in 2010 with the provocative and challenging title *Holiness: Is It Attainable Today?* (Ἡ ἁγιωσύνη εἶναι κατορθωτὴ σήμερα;), that has been translated here into English in its entirety. This is our way of offering yet another volume that conveys the aromatic fragrance of the Orthodox way of life to the contemporary man, whose mind may be searching for the perennial truth that brings joy and consolation, and whose soul may be thirsting for an authentic life in Christ.

In all of his writings, Fr. Moses is an eloquent and dynamic exponent of Orthodox Christianity. Not only is his literary style succinct and delightful, but, more importantly, his Orthodox theology is crystal clear, well balanced, and extraordinarily convincing for the existential condition of contemporary man. The theme and the premise of this beautiful book are truly inspiring and full of consolation and spiritual joy for those who would take up the struggle for an authentic spiritual life that is truly Orthodox and therefore also truly Christian.

The answer to the question in this book's title is a resounding "Yes!" Holiness is indeed attainable today, as the readers of this book will see for themselves. May this book be a blessing to all who will read it, as it has been a blessing for me to translate it into English for publication by Holy Cross Orthodox Press.

Fr. Peter A. Chamberas
Chaplain, Hellenic College and Holy Cross

Foreword

You must also read the life of the saint to the hearing of your child, and tell him, "Do you hear, my child, what your saint has accomplished? You too must do the same." By hearing such marvels, your child will become zealous and say to himself, "O, when will I too become like my saint?"[1]

Here is just one patristic reference that is close to us in time attesting to holiness as being achievable. St. Kosmas Aitolos, with whom I am associated in a rather special manner, dissects our spiritual indifference and sets down the ideal of holiness as the primary goal of education. This means that the desirable and achievable human "model" in the Christian family is the saint. This also means that the realism in the lives of the saints strips away our every possible excuse, making indefensible any negative assertion or the widespread notion that holiness is merely an hypothetical ideal, or a forgotten aspiration, or even a religious phenomenon of another time and place, or, finally, just a story about . . . saints.

The new reality in Christ, and the holiness of the believers, is already recorded with many references in the New Testament. Christians are called and properly referred to in their own right as saints. The phrase "to the saints" is found nineteen times, while the phrase "the saints" is found eight times. Here is one example: "To the saints who are in Ephesus, and faithful in Christ Jesus"

---

1. *St. Kosmas Aitolos*, ed. John Menounos (Athens: Tenos, 1984), 188.

(Eph 1:1). The separation, by divine grace, of the Christians from the world (from its mentality, its sinfulness) is denoted by this name, as is also the very goal of this new reality in Christ: "As He who called you is holy, you also be holy in all your conduct, because it is written, 'Be holy, for I am holy'" (1 Pet 1:15–16; cf. Lev 11:44, 45; 19:2; 20:7).

The calling to holiness is the very core of Christian Baptism and, because of this, of Christian self-consciousness as well. If, in our time, holiness has been exiled from our vision, this should neither surprise us nor even be a disadvantage to holiness. On the contrary, it only reflects the spiritual disaffection of us Christians who are being dragged along by the current of secularism and a rather diluted and blunted confession. Thus we are incapable of responding to our calling for holiness and making our name as saints correspond with our high calling in a manner that is consistent with apostolic tradition.

The purple-colored and undefiled testimony of the saints themselves certainly confirms that holiness is neither a vision nor a forgotten ideal, but rather a living, vital, and ever-present reality. And, in spite of the loud and alluring croaking to the contrary, the resounding and unashamed voice of Mt. Athos, the Holy Mountain where the Mother of God has trodden, reassures us, through its fragrant and myrrh-bearing experience of grace, of the holy struggle and the holy crown of those who have Christ in their heart, who love the saints, and who therefore respond indeed with self-denial to the high invitation of the Holy God. This same voice sends out a clarion call of the innermost and unquenchable (and often unknown) holy desire of each person to be made worthy, in Christ, "to become like the saints."

This present volume is the fourteenth in Athonite Flowers, a series of publications that spans the past twenty-five years, by the most-reverend *geronda* (elder) Moses of Mt. Athos, who has honored me with his request for this foreword and some editorial work. This volume contains six chapters, each relating to a particular aspect of holiness. The first chapter, "With All the Saints," recalls the saints and confirms that by imitating them we can securely commit our life to the Holy God. In the second chapter, "Holiness and the Saints," we have a very essential but also a clear theological and historical presentation of the subject, concluding with an extensive spiritual reference to our contemporary saint George Karslides. The third chapter, "Fools for Christ," presents an extraordinary form of asceticism and holiness. After all, holiness itself, at its most profound level, embodies the foolishness of the Cross. The fourth chapter, "The New Martyrs of Chios," highlights both the multitude of such martyrs on one island and how they were, in the power of their confession of faith, so very much like the first martyrs of the Church. It is truly an amazing example of youthful heroism and self-sacrificing holiness. Such a bouquet of holiness, coming from Mt. Athos, would be incomplete without the one who blossomed the Unfading Flower, the all-holy Theotokos and Lady of Mt. Athos, who is the subject of chapter five. The volume concludes with a final homily on the holy repentance of the holy prodigal son and the holy compassion and forgiveness of the holy and most-compassionate father. We pray that our most-compassionate Father will embrace all of us who may not be making spiritual progress and grant us the free gift of communion with His saints, now and always and unto the ages of ages. Amen.

Protopresbyter Athanasios Lagouros

1

With All the Saints

How were the saints sanctified? Were they a group of an extraordinary kind of people? Were they called to this purpose? Can we become holy? Are there any saints today? Could it be that holiness is only a phenomenon of the past?

All the saints had divine zeal, great love, and humility. Simple and pure hearts—which are also direct—possess kindness and cannot but love both God and man continuously, extravagantly, richly, wholeheartedly, and most fervently, without being obstructed at all by the various restrictions of life. All the saints left all things to follow Christ gladly, willingly, and honorably. They thus became elect vessels of His calling; they became His disciples, His children, His brothers and sisters, because they loved much.

The way of following Christ is not always strewn with rose petals. It is often an uphill climb, narrow, sorrowful, thorny, adventurous, and filled with many tribulations. It is not, my brothers and sisters, a journey of ease, security, rest, honor, and glory. It is, rather, my beloved, a way of martyrdom that is sometimes annihilating. It demands the taking up of the personal cross of a harsh daily routine of abstinence, exile, denial, obscurity, scorn, derision, and poverty. It is indeed a way of martyrdom that leads to the hill of Golgotha.

Our saints were all ascetics. Asceticism is given and taught by the Holy Gospel. The ascetic frame of mind prevailed in the hearts of all our saints. The ascetic struggle with patience and persistance is a real martyrdom and an authentic witness. A constant martyrdom of the conscience is the faithful observance of all the commandments of the Gospel. The observance of the commandments provides the inspired and holy virtues. In his most beautiful *Ascetic Discourses*, St. Basil the Great says, "Whoever desires the heavenly way of life becomes a struggling fellow soldier with the holy disciples of the Lord."

By living and experiencing their love for God and observing His divine will, the saints found boundless peace and blessedness. The saints passed through various ways. The saints are not a constant imitation of one by the other. Some lived their entire life in the desert, with various austere ways of life, whereas others lived in the cities, as married men or women, as shepherds, as workers. But they all loved both God and man without measure. They were all humble. They were certainly not all always "sanctified from their mother's womb" (cf. Jer 1:5). Many were led astray by sin, but they repented sincerely and were sanctified. Some chose remarkably austere ways to live their ascetic life: in confinement, in silence, in caves, in trees, on pillars, by burning their dwellings and constantly moving to another place, as fools for Christ. Were they thus irrational, strange, and extremist?

Even Christians, influenced by the quest for happiness, comfort, leisure, and a pleasant life, are unable to understand the extent of the love of these heroic persons, who sacrificed their entire lives and did not give their flesh the slightest ease, that they might become pleasing to their Lord and God. The total offering and dedication of a person to God is somewhat disconcerting to the many. For this reason, to justify perhaps their own laziness, they consider the saint peculiar, fanatical, and excessive. Have we not heard these things? Or, perhaps, are we too saying such things?

Even today they are not few who consider monasticism to be an entirely useless escape. In their argument they even assert that by staying in the world, the monks would be offering far more with the talents they have for the many needs of society today. To doubt the value of Orthodox monasticism—its history, value, and contribution—is certainly not a contemporary phenomenon. Of course, on the other hand we must say that those who consider absolutely that monasticism is the only way to perfection and salvation err seriously. In fact, St. Symeon the New Theologian, who was a monk, says, "Many followed the ascetic life, while others [followed] the communal life; others chose to shepherd and teach the people, while others chose other ways to live their life. I do not prefer any one of these ways of life, nor do I praise one and devalue another; but everywhere and always, in all works and activities, whoever works for God and according to the will of God is thrice blessed."

Our mother Orthodox Church never considered that the monks were not her genuine and beloved children. The monks did not hate the world but the worldly mentality, the worldliness and secularism of society. The monks worked for the world and shed rivers of tears in their prayers "for the salvation of the whole world." Often the world went to the desert to receive the spiritual counsel of an illumined ascetic. In times of great need, the monk himself would go out into the world, humbly and reverently, to help the suffering people of the world out of love. The Church did not appreciate monasticism in a one-dimensional manner, nor did she concern herself entirely with it. She did appreciate, however, the sincerity and the asceticism of the monks, and when it became necessary, she asked for their help and chose elect sons of the desert to serve her in high positions. It is entirely intolerable for monks to harbor even a small degree of superiority over those brothers and sisters in the world who are piously struggling in a godly way.

Holiness, as we have said other times as well, is the major purpose of human life on earth. This is the primary reason why we all exist and live. If we do not succeed in this, then surely we have failed in a major way. Our Lord Jesus Christ is holiness itself. He became incarnate for this reason and opened the way for our deification. Holiness is not isolation and has no loneliness.

Holiness is a beautiful and sacred relationship. It is a relationship with God, the source of holiness itself, which sanctifies the human person and makes him into an image of meekness, into a divine person. There is no other holiness besides the one granted by God Himself to His faithful servants. Holiness is not a discovery, an advantage, a private achievement, an individual success, a moral acquisition, or the attainment of some record in athletics or in some other championship. Holiness is grace and a blessing from God; it is participation and communion and a fellowship with others. The saints are not lights in themselves; they receive their light from another source. The saints do not save; they only intercede. All the saints lead us to Christ. If we are permitted to say it, the various Protestants who do not honor the saints and the all-holy Theotokos are most unfortunate. The saints share by grace and participation in the holiness of God.

Holiness is entrance into paradise, a foretaste of the ineffable joy of the eternal kingdom of heaven. Holiness is the acceptance of the invitation that God extends to man. The saint is an individual who becomes a person and is recorded on the roster of the heavenly kingdom. This invitation is of course extended to all. The Lord says, "You shall be holy, for I the Lord your God am holy" (Lev 19:2). A saint is one wholesome and complete personality who lives to love, to accept the divine mercy, to do what is good, and to glorify God.

A saint cannot be peculiar, morose, eccentric, voluptuous, selfish, vainglorious, or ambitious. A saint is distinguished, as we said, by his humility and love. A saint will preserve the elements of his character and personality, that is to say, if he is an introvert or extrovert, a sociable or a withdrawn person. With the grace of God, however, one can overcome his weaknesses and his own desires. He comes and goes motivated by the Holy Spirit.

Moreover, we must simply say that holiness is never an occasional tendency or inclination, or what we may call intense religiosity. Holiness is not a fragmentary and partial attribute of man. It is, rather, an exceptional love for God, a faithful and steadfast journey upon the way of the sacred gospel and the tradition of the Church. The evangelic and traditional man, the one who is ecclesial and a Christian, does not live in a world of his own, doing whatever comes into his own mind, originating and improvising, but instead is living the authentic way of life and thus is being saved, restored, redeemed, and sanctified. A modernist—one who is disobedient, arbitrary, self-sufficient, eccentric, an individualist, an antitraditional man—is not only not a saint, but is one who does not even touch the predetermined fringes of holiness marked out by the blood of Christ and the martyrs.

Holiness, then, is the way of evangelical perfection. It constitutes, we repeat, a relationship of love and communion with the living Christ. It is the experience of the liturgical expression "And our whole life [we commit] to Christ our God." It is the giving of our entire life, our thought, and our very being to Christ. It is the total, unreserved, and uncalculated trust and self-offering of our whole being to the Creator of the entire universe.

Holiness is never a static condition, a passive state of nirvana, a blessed rest and delight in gains and victories, but is rather a constant humble struggle, a permanent effort, an ongoing contest for the combatant to steadily and discretely maintain his relationship with Jesus Christ, his neighbor, and himself. In a contest one will either lose or win. Thus even saints may fall. This is why constant vigilance is needed to maintain wakefulness and an upward and upright extension of the soul. The wiles of the devil are most cunning and well positioned for all. Even a saint can fall again, fail, and go wrong. But when he humbles himself, he can once again gain grace.

Many often pose the question: Is holiness attainable today? Is holiness perhaps something untouchable, unattainable, and impossible for the present time? Is it even an exaggeration to be talking about something like this? Indeed, people today have other priorities, perspectives, and goals. They think about other things, study other things, and are concerned and struggle over other things. For many, the thought of holiness does not even cross their mind. Even for Christians, holiness is considered something from the past, something outmoded that is not for contemporary people. A considerable number of people see holiness as something hidden far away from modern society. The so-called common opinion has another understanding. If the subject of holiness were to be posed as a question in a public poll, many people would simply pass us by and smile condescendingly. The devil has done his work well; he has created a general and pervasive indifference to the subject of holiness in our life.

The saints are the great, courageous, daring heroes of history. They are the ones who stood apart from the masses and refused to be assimilated; they mocked materialism and bypassed the prevailing fashion, which they resisted strenuously and fearlessly. The many, of course, did not understand the saints and gave them a bad name, wanting thus to marginalize and prevent them from becoming a nuisance. Unfortunately, the world "lies in evil" and has other criteria. Christ is asking for all of our love. The saints gave it to Him. The relationship of the saints with Christ is one of great love and dedication. This is not understood by the world, and is therefore misunderstood. Most people usually misunderstood the saints. The people, therefore, have a different opinion, judgment, and appreciation of the saints. Thus holiness has a cost attached to it. The saints themselves, however, are not afraid of this cost. Their love makes them capable of enduring everything; they can forgive from the heart both those who would abuse them and those who would crucify them.

Sometimes worldly people will confront a saint and consider him to be insane. St. Anthony, a long time ago, had foretold that the insane would look even upon a rational man and consider him to be insane. If not confronted in this way, the saints are at least considered to be peculiar, otherworldly, and backward, and are therefore rejected. The saints, however, do not hate such people and are not disconcerted by rejection. Sometimes the saints are even glad that people do not honor them. Other times they are sad about the spiritual insensitivity and the deliberate misunderstanding of the people. The saints will simply disturb, with only their presence, those who are complacently slothful, those who are comfortable in multiple ways, and those who are at ease in their procrastination, their transfer of responsibility, and their indifferent self-justification by saying, "Everyone is doing it" and "I will not be the one to draw the snake out of its hole."

The logic of these justifications and the constant comparison with those who are worse off is a considerably easy solution. It helps the conscience to slumber blessedly in the sleep of those who presume themselves righteous. The logic of the world is indeed different; it calculates constantly its own interest and advantage, its selfishness, its gain, its ease and how it alone will be served. In the life of the saint, other very different elements prevail: self-sacrifice, good works, selflessness, tolerance, forgiveness, patience, and hope. The worldly person does not easily give up his creature comforts. Unfortunately, this worldly spirit has penetrated even into the life of Christians. The opinion prevails that it is not possible to observe the whole evangelic way of life today. Thus the gospel is utilized in a fragmentary, utilitarian manner, without "too many austere elements." There are not a few Christians who are simply satisfied with a certain "discounted" spiritual life, one that is lacking the indispensable evangelical consistency and is merely a typical and dutifully proper spiritual life that only seems to be progressive and pleasing to God.

The irrationality of the world considers irrational the rationality of God. Thus the saints are considered to be irrational, incomprehensible, extremists. You can understand the magnitude of this deception. We cannot even find a point of reference and come to an understanding, at least, on the very basic elements. The endless lines of pious anchorites, abandoning the world for the desert, to live there the gospel in its fullness and to reject any compromise with the worldly mentality, did not cease to pray with tears for the repentance and the salvation of the world. Their departure from the world was to avoid the bonds of a life filled with many cares, much noise, and a multitude of anxieties.

The strong, unwavering, fervent faith of all the saints was their invincible weapon. Such faith is also a great love that unites the believer with God. St. Nicholas Kabasilas says that as the eye was fashioned to enjoy the light and the ear to hear beautiful sounds, man also was created to be united with God. St. Augustine says that man will not find peace and quiet until he is united with God. The most profound being of man will always be seeking God. The invincible desire of every man is holiness. God Himself implanted in the heart of man this unceasing divine yearning, which the Holy Fathers have named *divine eros*. Having this great love within them, the saints endured unbearably horrific sufferings, imprisonments, tortures, exiles, condemnations, calumnies, threats, persecutions, injustices, blasphemies, ridicules, and pillages. The saints were indeed in love with Christ.

The extraordinary monastic saint Isaac the Syrian says characteristically, "When the love of God kindles the heart of one who is struggling, then he cannot draw his heart away to be separated from Him. He dispels from within every fear and becomes ecstatic. The power that limits his rationality vanishes. He becomes as if irrational, and even death itself appears joyful. He is not in heaven, but imagines being there." St. John Chrysostom himself continues in the same vein: "Whoever has been wounded by the unceasing *divine eros* sees the present world differently and considers the entire present life as a shadow, a dream, and a fantasy."

All the saints of our Church are the ones who "fought the good fight . . . [and] kept the faith" (2 Tim 4:7). The saints are the gloriously triumphant warriors and impeccable confessors. They are the ones who were visited by the Holy Spirit and were sanctified. They are not simply the good, the congenial, the noble, the smiling, the moral, but the images of Christ. They are the ones who remain inseparably united with Christ; they reveal Christ to the world and lead the world to Christ. The saints reassure us that the gospel is indeed accessible and attainable at all times and to us as well, if we only will it and struggle to be united with Christ. The saints, by accepting Christ in their life unreservedly, become Christians, bearers of Christ, and Christ is formed in them. Thus they witness to Him, confess Him, preach Him, and present Him always and everywhere. They cannot live without Christ; He is everything to them.

From time to time opportunities to confess Christ are given to us too. Sometimes we do so directly and happily, other times with difficulty, and again other times not at all, out of fear or shame. One who is truly a believer in Christ will confess Him always without fear, because he is constantly living in repentance and in humility. He may feel powerless, but his complete trust in Christ empowers him abundantly. He confesses Christ, who lives within him. Sometimes we have difficulty in confessing Christ even to those who are very close and dear to us. At such times, according to the Gospel, "a man's enemies will be those of his own household" (Matt 10:36). It so happens that our people do not understand us, but we also do not make any effort to speak to them discreetly about Christ. Or perhaps we sometimes even go to the opposite extreme. We talk to them so very much about Christ that in the end we tire them, satiate them, and pressure and annoy them so much that they do not even want to hear anything about Christ. We can never pressure anyone, assume a commanding authority over him, or threaten him—even our closest relative—to follow Christ.

Christ is freedom and love. He extends an invitation, and does not demand and extort. We are called to inspire people in their love for Christ. If man is self-imprisoned in the strong bonds of his ego, he suffers from egotism, individualism, vanity, and pride, and has a hard time loving others and much more so God Himself. Thus he also has difficulty in confessing Him before people. If one does not confess, it means that he also does not love. One who does not love is self-condemned in a cold loneliness that will begin in this life and continue into the eternal one. The egotist, who only loves himself, will also experience the love of God—but as a burning fire that he cannot endure and does not want, because it is a fire that censures and burns him.

The saint entrusts his entire life completely into the hands of God, humbly and willingly, and in this way it is empowered, strengthened, and fortified, even when the people do not honor him and consider him to be in last place. However, as the Gospel says, those who here are in last place will be in first place there

(Matt 19:30; 20:16; Mark 10:31). The spiritual criteria of the Gospel are indeed different. Here, in this world, many are living for the sake of the first seats of honor, the applause, the accolades, the rewards, and the prestige, as they marvel at themselves and are glad seeing themselves in first place. When these people are mocked, they in turn mock others. They live to be applauded and praised, provoking others, seeking and begging for honors, and while imagining themselves in first place, they are indeed in last.

The saints in this world were always the ones who "had nothing" but who, for God and in God, "had everything." The saints are the wealthy poor, the ones, as we said, who entrusted themselves entirely to God. God glorifies the saints, and they are the ones who are recognized by the conscience and the fullness of the Church. The Church officially recognizes and determines the month and the day on which to honor a saint, who is already being honored as such by faithful people. The saints, obeying the calls of the all-powerful Holy Spirit, who enacts and fulfills all things, direct with their life and teaching the ecclesial body of the Church. Their lives and teachings constitute the ecclesial word of God. Their presence in the world is a presence of the living Christ.

Only the Orthodox Church bears true saints to this day. The truth of the Church is preserved even in the smallest minorities. This is the proof that even today, a time of great apostasy, our Church produces saints, known and unknown, small and great. In spite of the fearful mistakes of some representatives of the Church—mistakes for which we are all deeply sorrowful, because these representatives forgot the purpose of their dedication and loved the "gold" more than Christ and the flesh more than the spirit—there is, nevertheless, hidden holiness in the desert and in the world.

The saints do not grow old, do not wear out, do not tire in helping all those who ask with faith—those who are sick, in need, in trouble, those with problems, the disillusioned, the unfortunate, those who are suffering and fearful. We reverence their honorable, grace-filled relics and their miraculous icons, and they come to our aid. Their divine biographies teach us, inspire us, benefit us, console us, strengthen us, empower us, and encourage us. Many of them were like us, and a considerable number of them were in far more difficult or even worse circumstances than we are, and yet they did not give up or yield in their struggle. They strengthen us and console us most exceptionally.

Today there are Christians who love the saints, who study their lives, go to their festivals, light their vigil lamps, reverence their holy icons, and dedicate in their honor churches, chapels, icons, vigil lamps, sweet breads, offering breads, *kollyva*, and so forth. There are also those who do not love the saints—and we are not talking about the atheists, the irreverent, or the irreligious—but those who are influenced by rationalism, by a certain rationalistic modern theology that considers all such things as infirmities of the spirit and a form of nontheological popular piety. Unfortunately, a large portion of the Christian world has not fully understood the tremendous value and significance of the saints in our life.

The reverence, piety, and fervency of those faithful who love the saints has certainly not disappeared in our days. You see homes filled with holy icons, with a vigil lamp or a candle constantly burning; you see simple grandmothers speaking to you with tears about the marvelous appearance of the saints in their lives; you see pious people hoping, through the intercessions of the saints and the Theotokos, for their salvation and their entrance into paradise. Those who love the saints are those who even today seek out the real saints for support and benefit. They do not create the saints in their imagination, nor do they follow those God-mocking pseudo-saints, but they do bow before true and authentic holiness. Those who love the saints are the most elect part of the congregation in the parishes. They continue the tradition; they reverently honor the feast days of our saints; they are not easily scandalized by the pseudo-saints; they are not influenced and tossed to and fro by the ecclesiastical scandals that are real or those that are not. When they find themselves in difficult circumstances, as with our neighboring people of the same faith under totalitarian regimes, they endure courageously, hopefully, and victoriously.

The saints remain always humble because they have the certain conviction that whatever good they have is granted to them from above; it is not their own achievement. Thus the saints cannot brag, cannot have any pride in themselves, and cannot boast of their gifts, because these gifts are granted to them by the Father of lights. Our saints, having full awareness of their gift, attribute every glory, honor, and reverence to God, who is the true and ultimate gift giver. As people praise them, the saints in turn praise the Benevolent God, who is the source of every good thing. As God sees a person becoming more humble, the more He showers him with blessings and grace, since it is always to the humble that grace is given (cf. Jas 4:6; Prov 3:34). Someone who may be charismatic but who uses his gift for his own glory and selfish benefit will surely quickly lose it and be pitifully exposed to those he may be exploiting. Even in this life such a person will be troubled, confused, and wretched, whereas in the future life there will be eternal torment awaiting him.

My beloved friends, there is an abundance of hidden holiness even in our own difficult times. This holiness is found not only in the life of insignificant, unknown, obscure monks in the deserts and in the cenobitic monasteries, but also in the world. There are spouses who endure with long-suffering their unstable and prodigal spouses, who may be harsh alcoholics, all-night gamblers, totally resigned to their passions and apparently incapable of spiritual progress. These devout spouses do not take refuge in divorce, but endure and hope and pray, and do not give up the struggle to provide, at least, good nurturing for their children. This particular stance of the mother teaches the children, and it becomes an excellent example and motivation toward virtue. This heroic stance may, in time, even turn the violent spouse around, and in the end will certainly offer her the crown of patience for this long (and often lifelong) martyrdom. We too have known such rare heroines, who for many years secretly lived a horrible martyrdom in silence, patience, prayer, tears, and humility, always trusting and hoping in God. How can God not grant grace to such beautiful souls?

You see then that holiness has many aspects. The people in the world will not be judged because they do not offer much prayer, even though there are some who pray more than the monks do. St. John Chrysostom says, "The laypeople will be saved by their charitable love." Charity reveals a humble soul that knows how to love. In our most cunning and alluring times, whoever humbles himself, whoever practices self-control, whoever purifies himself, and whoever is honorable, sincere, just, and prudent will have much reward from heaven. The discreet elders say that what is important in the spiritual life is not the place (τόπος) but the manner (τρόπος). It is possible for an ascetic to be in the deepest desert and to be suffering from worldly thoughts, while someone in the city may be truly humble and serene. The same kind of demon says to the married person to abandon his family and go to the monastery, because only there will he be saved, and to the monk he says to go to the world and stay there permanently to be saved. Let us increase our love for Christ on a daily basis, and, as Geronda Porphyrios Kausokalyvites used to say, we can be anywhere at all and still live a perfectly holy life.

Undoubtedly, the greatest treasure in the world is the presence of the saints. These are people who gave their entire life to Christ, without holding back anything for themselves. The ascetic struggle cleansed them, and holy repentance illumined them. The constant sense of their sinfulness empowered them with humility. The saints are fragrant vessels of the Spirit: permanent dwellings of the Holy Spirit and sources of graceful gifts. They themselves, however, believed firmly that they were the most sinful persons.

The blessed geronda Paisios the Haghiorite, when visited by people with photographic cameras and recording machines, used to say gracefully, "I am no worthy sight to behold, nor a museum or a zoological garden." Geronda Porphyrios, who had the proven gift of foresight and certainly of insight, used to say, "People come and see me, thinking that I am saintly, but I know that I am the most sinful man in the world!" People who are vainglorious tend to seek praise, but the saints do not enjoy such applause. Their joy is to please the Lord. The saints and the virtuous and saintly elders are rather saddened when people approach them as if they are magicians, gurus, and doers of marvels. The secular and worldly people find it hard to be humbled, to endure their problem, to kneel down, to weep, to pray without ceasing. They seek for solutions that are direct, uninterrupted, effortless, easy, and quick. They want to know their fate, their future, and, in that assurance, continue their way of life; they are not really looking to benefit spiritually and to repent. Those who approach the elders in this manner depart in disappointment, because no serious elder is concerned with worldly future successes and material gains. The gifts of grace are given and utilized only for the salvation of the soul.

Holiness exists, of course, but it is not spread out everywhere. It has its presuppositions; it requires the proper climate to be developed and to flourish. When seeking but not finding any saints, let us not create our own! We will appreciate our spiritual father, respect him, and obey him, but we are not the ones to place upon him the crown of glory. Let us not be in a hurry, let us not exaggerate, and let us not act sentimentally, superficially, and offhandedly in such serious matters.

Before a saint we stand reverently, humbly, silently, prayerfully. Let us allow him to speak to us, to tell us in a better way whatever God illumines him to tell us. He will advise us of what is necessary for our salvation. Let us not start with endless questions. Let us not tire him with unnecessary things. He will understand much with the few things we say to him. Let us not extend ourselves into myriad details concerning our problems. Let us not assume that this is the opportunity for him to solve all of our problems. When we allow the saints to speak on their own terms, they will be thus enabled to help us in a much more effective way. This way they will benefit us more, will console us and strengthen us, and we will then depart with peace and joy.

When someone goes to the elders, asking about sublime theoretical subjects when he has not yet established a firm and basic spiritual infrastructure in his soul, this is a vainglorious undertaking. It is in fact gross irreverence to be seeking information about the higher levels of the virtues when we have long ago neglected the basic needs of our soul. What should we say, then? Simply say, "Geronda, tell me something for my salvation." This suffices. This expresses everything necessary. We have spoken before about the pseudo-saint and the pseudo-charismatic in clerical garb who appears in our seductive times. People in their agonized seeking or in their unbearable pain will stumble upon these deceivers and be distressed. This is why great care and attention are needed. Error and deception have great power and abundant demonic energy to lead astray, to imprison, and to create ugly and unhealthy conditions, which then become extremely difficult to heal.

May the saints deliver us from such dangerous circumstances. According to the elder Justin Popovich,

> The saints are the more perfected Christians, because they have been sanctified to the highest possible degree by the asceticism of faith in the resurrected and eternally living Lord Jesus Christ . . . The lives of the saints are none other than the life of Christ the Savior, repeated in each saint, more or less and in one way or another. Or, more precisely, it is the life of Christ extended and perpetuated in space and time by the saints. And this life is the life of the incarnate God the Logos, the God-Man Jesus, who became man for this very reason, that He as man might grant and transmit His divine life to us, and in this way might sanctify and immortalize and eternalize with His life as God our own human life upon earth.

My beloved brothers and sisters, I will conclude my humble remarks with these beautiful words of St. Silouan the Athonite about the saints: "The saints, through their love, embrace the whole world in the Holy Spirit. They can see and understand how we are exhausted by sorrows, how our hearts are dried up, how carelessness has dissipated our souls. And because of this awareness, they intercede for us without ceasing before God. The saints rejoice over our repentance and grieve whenever people abandon

God and resemble the irrational creatures. The saints grieve because people live upon earth, without knowing that if they only loved one another, there would be upon earth freedom from sin."

St. Silouan knows very well what he is saying. The saints love us and stand by us in many and diverse ways, but especially with their ceaseless intercessions. Let us not grieve them, therefore, with our sins. Let us have true and sincere repentance so that we may bring joy not only to the saints, but also to the Lord Himself. Amen.

2

HOLINESS AND THE SAINTS

IN OUR DAY, GLORY BE TO GOD, there are many books in circulation about older and newer saints, and the people indeed love them in particular. There are also in circulation beautiful biographies of contemporary virtuous elders. Allow me to say that much has been written and said, but I am afraid that we love to hear about them in a rather light literary way, without deciding to make some significant change in our life.

There is one main goal of human life upon earth: to know God, to sanctify and to be sanctified. God Himself has said, "Be holy as I am holy." God is the only truly holy one, holiness itself and goodness itself. My beloved brothers and sisters, our failure to achieve this goal in our life is indeed the greatest tragedy of man. The only saint, then, is God. This is why we say in every Divine Liturgy, "One is holy, one is Lord, Jesus Christ, to the glory of God the Father." Holy means to be pure, clean, immaculate, and separated from anything sinful. Holiness is not contagious, but it is achievable. By struggling humbly, patiently, and persistently, by observing the divine commandments and being motivated by love, we can approach God and be thus cleansed, illumined, and deified.

Generally speaking, saints are all those who are baptized as Orthodox Christians and have received the Holy Spirit in their Baptism. They thus believe firmly in Christ as Savior and Redeemer of the world, and are aware of His presence in the world. Moreover, they believe in eternal life, the Second Coming of the Lord (which will take place at a time that no human knows), and they live a pure and immaculate life. Usually there is a mistaken impression about holiness, even among the faithful. People think that a saint is someone extraterrestrial, with superhuman powers, someone who is otherworldly, antisocial, strange, and peculiar in form and manner of life. Such an opinion, of course, is completely out of place and wrong. The saints do not hate the world, they do not avoid pain, they are not antisocial, and they are not isolated. They live within the pulse of daily life but are not influenced by the evil of the world, because they are firmly united with Christ. The saint is struggling both within and outside of the world, by hating the worldly mentality and way of life, and by loving all human beings. Society is the stadium in which the Christian struggles to achieve the fervent virtues.

A saint will preserve, strengthen, bless, and grace the world. In an exceptional way, a saint loves Christ, the Church, virtue, and his neighbor. He always hopes in divine help, assistance, blessing, illumination, and grace. He has complete awareness of his sinfulness, unworthiness, and insignificance. He constantly appeals for divine mercy. He sees what we have been created for, not where we have fallen. In problems, sufferings, and temptations, he sees God's instructive presence, the divine justice, and the beneficial intervention of heaven for our salvation. A saint does not tire easily, is never disillusioned, and has entrusted his whole being to God. Thus the saint has the best security, the greatest peace, abundant rest, fearlessness, serenity, calmness, and gladness. The saint surpasses the many difficulties of life with his absolute trust in God. He never regrets his destiny and does not complain, because he is genuinely humble.

The saints do not have external distinguishing marks that would separate them and set them apart. They go through the world quietly, unobserved; they live simply, peacefully, and serenely. They do not have particular dwellings, clothing, food, vocabulary, and high acquaintances. They live in the world as if out of the world, and out of the world as if in the world. They have nothing, and yet one might say with St. Paul that they have all things (2 Cor 6:10). They have a country, but they live as if sojourners. With all they are friendly, and with all strangers, according to St. Isaac the Syrian. They have flesh, but one would think that they are incorporeal. They live on earth and are citizens of heaven. They love all, but many are they who persecute them. Their poverty is for them abundance and riches. The dishonorable things done to them are considered to be honors, and the accusations praises. The saints are slandered, ridiculed, and wronged, and yet they rejoice, pray, bless, and forgive.

The saints are constantly struggling, without interruption. They struggle to overcome the passions, to acquire the virtues, to attain dispassion, and to be maintained in this state, by the grace of God. No saint ever said that he was a saint. St. Gregory of Nyssa says that holiness is a perfection that does not have an end. A good person alone cannot be identified with a saint. Not all of the good people will be saved. Not all the ethical people will enter paradise. Of the ten virgins, only five were saved. To be a good person is one thing, but it is quite another to be saved, to be a saint. These must not be confused. We must emphasize and underline this, because often there are misunderstandings, misinterpretations, and inappropriate comparisons.

A real saint is the salt of a society; he gives it taste, fragrance, grace, and joy. A true saint is a blessing, a graceful gift, an adornment, and an image of God. A saint can be eloquent in his silence. He preaches with his luminous example and way of life. He holds no puffed-up opinion about himself; he makes no demands, he expects no human honor or praise, and he does not seek to convince anyone. He feels that he is the most sinful person, the last in line. If he should believe for even an instant that he is something different and that he is something more than the others, this will be a terribly dangerous entrapment that will sooner or later destroy him.

A cunning deception is that of pseudo-holiness. This is for one to think and believe that he is a saint, for one to imagine that he has visions and signs and to deceive the simple and gullible. Such deceivers bear great responsibility themselves, because such mocking of God is a serious sin, but this responsibility is also borne by those who superficially and without a struggle are constantly seeking to find "saints" who will solve their problems directly, who will relieve them from the need for a struggle and will bring about—suddenly and effortlessly—happiness, prosperity, ease, and rest. May God protect us from such pseudo-saints. This is clearly a matter of those who deceive and those who are being deceived (2 Tim 3:13).

According to St. John of Damascus, the great dogmatic theologian of our Church, there is at the summit of holiness, after the Holy Trinity, the more-than-holy—the all-holy—Theotokos, who is above all the saints. The Virgin Mary is the constant, extraordinary prototype of holiness. She is the inspiration, the hope, and the consolation for all Christians of all the ages. She is the Mother of both God and the faithful people. She is the all-immaculate queen of all, the most-beautiful provider of consolation, mercy, and freedom; the one who is full of grace; the one who is all-pure, more honorable than the cherubim and beyond compare more glorious than the seraphim. Her powerful mediation, her constant intercession and her eager cooperative assistance, contributes significantly on the way to our holiness. This is why the writers of hymns and the chanters of hymns praise her without ceasing.

Elect saints of our Church are all the righteous and prophets of the Old Testament, from the patriarch Abraham all the way down to the glorious and honorable St. John the Baptist. Then come the holy apostles and disciples of the Lord, the twelve and the seventy; the evangelists; and the greatest missionary of all ages, the divine St. Paul, "the mouthpiece of God," as St. John Chrysostom calls him.

The martyrs are particularly beloved children of God. A considerable number of them could have avoided martyrdom by hiding or pretending, but they did no such thing. The opportunity was given to them to save their body by denying temporarily (or not so temporarily) their faith, but they did not even think of this at all. Their great love for Christ made them fearless, courageous, unsusceptible to terror, indifferent to pain, and unintimidated even by death itself. They endured persecutions, horrible tortures, vilifications, imprisonments, deprivations, sufferings, and unimaginable tribulations. Their blood, shed for Christ's sake, endowed them with the purple robe of royalty and the bright crown of sanctity. This is why, in the case of martyrs, our Church does not use any particular process to recognize their holiness.

We have old martyrs from the past and new martyrs from more recent times. We have apostolic martyrs such as Peter and Paul, the leaders of the apostles. We have martyrs from among the clergy, the hieromartyrs, such as Stephen, the first martyr and archdeacon, and St. Haralampos, who was martyred at the age of 113, and St. Kosmas the equal-to-the-apostles; we have bishops such as St. Ignatius the God-bearer, St. Polycarp of Smyrna, St. Antipas of Pergamon, and St. Eleftherios; we have patriarchs such as St. Gregory V and many others. We also have great military martyrs such as Sts. George, Demetrios, Menas, and the two Theodores. We have female virgin martyrs such as Barbara, Kyriake, and Marina. We have monastic female virgin martyrs such as Paraskeve, Philothei the Athenian, and many others.

The glorious cloud of new martyrs, those martyrs of Christ who were martyred after the Fall of Constantinople in 1453, came from various regions and various types of work, and were of various ages: Chrysostom of Smyrna, George of Yiannena, Constantine of Hydra, Nicholas of Metsovo, and many others.

Continuators of the martyrdom of blood were the *hosioi*, the voluntary martyrs of the conscience, the martyrs of obedience, the martyrs of great asceticism, the martyrs of an entire lifetime, the faithful followers, even unto death, of the narrow and sorrowful ascetic way. And there are also those extraordinary saints who lived in confinement, on pillars, in trees, in caves, and in total poverty and abandonment, without dwellings or clothing or any other possessions; and, of course, the saints of Mt. Athos, the Holy Mountain. Among the monastic saints, we mention a mere sampling: St. Antonios, St. Theodosios the Cenobiarch, St. Efthymios, St. Pachomios, St. Athanasios the Athonite, St. Seraphim of Sarov.

Another category of saints is that of those who undauntedly confessed the faith before kings and tyrants but who did not end their life in martyrdom, instead enduring many tribulations: St. Chariton, St. Maximos the Confessor, St. Theophanes the Graptos, St. Theodore the Studite, and others.

The God-bearing Fathers of the Church include, among many others, St. Athanasios the Great; St. John the Merciful of Alexandria; St. Nicholas of Myra in Lycia; St. Spyridon the Wonderworker; and the three luminaries of the trihypostatic divinity, the Three Hierarchs: St. John Chrysostom, St. Basil the Great, and St. Gregory the Theologian.

In our own time, which we readily criticize, we have a multitude of saints, men and women, from the entire Orthodox world and throughout the twentieth century, who are luminous examples and the extension of Christ throughout the ages, as the saintly elder Justin Popovich used to say. All of these saints confirm and reassure us that the gospel is achievable and applicable in our own time. These new saints inspire, motivate, provide examples, and challenge us, and, of course, they intercede for us.

Here is a partial list as a mere sampling: Parthenios of the Monastery of Koudouma (+1905) and his brother Eumenios (+1920); Methodia of Kimolo (+1908); John of Kronstadt (+1908); Nicholas the Illuminator of Japan (+1912); Eudokimos the Iberite (+1913); Maximos of Poland (+1914); Aristokles the Athonite (+1918); Nectarios of Pentapolis the Wonderworker (+1920); the hieromartyrs Euthymios of Tilos (+1921), Chrysostom of Smyrna (+1922), Gregory of Kydonia (+1922), Ambrosios of Moschonesia (+1922), Gabriel and Arcadios the Iberites (+1923), Arsenios the Cappadocian (+1924), Nectarios of Optina (+1928); Nicholas Planas of Athens (+1932); Alexios the Russian (+1934); Silouan the Athonite (+1938); the Polish hieromartyrs Ignatios (+1943), Paul (+1943), Sergios (+1943), Peter (+1944), Leon (+1944), Nicholas (+1944), and Basil (+1945); Savvas of Kalymnos (+1948); Nicholas of Zitse and Ochrid (+1956); George Karslides (+1959); Anthimos of Chios (+1960); Luke of Crimea (+1961); Kouxa of Odessa (+1964); John Maximovitch (+1966); Philoumenos of Jerusalem (+1979); plus a great multitude of new martyrs in Russia, Albania, Serbia, Romania, Bulgaria, and Turkey.

During the twentieth century we also had a great, long, and significant line of very virtuous elders and abbesses. On Mt. Athos alone during the twentieth century, we had 450 elders, about whom we have been preparing for a long time now a collective work. Such saintly personalities existed in all of Greece and throughout the Orthodox world. In what follows we will refer briefly to one such saintly personality, Elder Hieronymos of Simonos Petra (+1957), whose biography we have been preparing for years now. It was the habit of Abbot Hieronemos of Simonos Petra to sleep a little on a bench or on chair. He used to say, "For a monk it should suffice that he is even under a protective cover." They said about him that he had consumed more lamp oil during his endless readings and studies than he had drunk water throughout his life. When his brothers criticized him for embezzlement, even though he was well aware of the guilty parties, his long-suffering forbearance did not permit him to reveal them; rather, he simply said to those who questioned him, "Maybe St. Simon knows . . . Perhaps he needed the money and took it." He endured exile without complaint. He served as a humble muleteer in the Monastery of Koutloumousiou. He stayed for a period of time in a coal storage space in the area of Kausokalyvia. He passed from the Metochion (Dependency) of St. Haralampos in Thessalonike and ended up in the Metochion of the Ascension in Athens. He never ceased praying fervently for his accusers and his slanderers. At the end of his constant struggles to prove his love for God, he received the heavenly graces of discretion, insight, and foresight. He was made worthy to serve the Divine Liturgy with angels and to not be standing on solid ground when celebrating the Liturgy. His spiritual children speak of him with sacred awe and about the miracles of his most fervent prayers. The moment of his death came when he was praying and thanking God for the great gift of his frequent illnesses.

For those who appreciate numbers, allow me to share some with you: At the age of seventeen he came to Simonos Petra from Reiz-Dere in Asia Minor. After four and a half years as a novice, he was tonsured as a monk of the great schema by the well-known abbot Neophytos from Alatsata. For a period of over forty-three years, he did not sleep in a bed. For sixty-nine years he wore the honored monastic cassock, and always used it as a service apron for his brothers. His spiritual children number into the tens of hundreds. His letters of consolation have been estimated to be about ten thousand. On a daily basis he commemorated over two thousand five hundred names of living and deceased persons at the Proskomide. After his saintly repose they found in his drawer seven drachmas that perhaps he did not have a chance to hand out to his poor friends, in whose doorways he would secretly leave his charity at night. He reposed in the Lord at the age of eighty-six on January 7, 1957. Thousands of people were at his funeral, many of them relating with tears many marvelous events in his lifetime. He was buried behind the holy altar of the Church of the Ascension, the *metochion* in Byrona, Athens, of the Athonite Monastery of Simonos Petra.

Fr. Hieronymos served the *metochion* from 1931 as its steward. He helped and benefitted thousands of souls. With this exceptional "arithmetic," how could his blessed relics not be fragrant? When they were transferred in 1965, I, a child then, followed the events with great awe and emotion, not knowing then that after two decades I would be a monk in his monastery and eventually his biographer. My blessed mother had him as her spiritual father.

Metropolitan Nicholas of Mesogaias and Laurentikes, while living at the *metochion*, wrote the following about Fr. Hieronymos: "He was an earthly angel, a heavenly man. He was a virtuous man that censured you. You were a sinful man and he comforted you. You loved him and he distanced you. You created temptations for him and he did not avoid you. You praised him and he reproached you. You wronged him and he refused to be justified. Often he exuded a sweet fragrance. He was so contrite and compunctious that almost always during the reading of the Gospel his voice would break and his eyes would shed tears. He enjoyed meeting the souls of those he commemorated. His participation in the divine worship transfigured him into an angel."

In what follows, my beloved, I shall tell you about a recently recognized saint of our Church, the *hosios* George Karslides, whose humble biographer I was again blessed to be, as I was blessed to include new information about his life that has come to light. This saint was born in Argyroupolis of Pontos, a land that nurtures saints, in 1901. He became an orphan at an early age, and his most pious grandmother assumed his upbringing. Once when he was visiting his brother's house, a beggar came to ask for charity. Then George went with a dish to the area where food was stored and gave him a portion of flour. When his sister-in-law found out about it, she scolded him severely. After this he left and went to be a shepherd of sheep for a Turk. One day while caring for the sheep, he saw three men chanting most beautifully. He suddenly lost sight of them and began to weep for the loss. He returned home in tears. After some time his employer found out the reason for his tears and led him down into a secret crypt; there George encountered the icon of the Three Holy Hierarchs and recognized them. The Turk was actually a crypto-Christian, who guided George to go to a monastery.

At the age of only eight, George arrived at the monastery and there learned to read and write in the Georgian language. In 1917, with the revolution in Russia, the atheists were pressuring the monks to renounce their faith. Those who refused to comply were shot to death. Young George was also shot in the chest, but the bullet lodged in the medallion he was wearing, which had been given to him by his uncle, a bishop. The other bullets hit him in the legs and left him seriously injured. He suffered throughout his life from the wounds inflicted upon his body by the atheists.

With the help of the all-holy Theotokos and the saints, he stayed alive. Rarely was he healthy. He lived to serve the Divine Liturgy, to pray, to offer charity, to hear confessions, and to help and support others. His words and counsels were well remembered by many and kept as a sacred tradition. This blessed man also had discretion, insight, and foresight.

One of his spiritual daughters said, "We had gone for the first time to make our confession. We did not speak. He held an opened book and would ask us, 'Have you done this? Have you done that?' When he had finished, he told me, 'Do not be unjust to the orphan child that lives alone in the house next door where you hang the tobacco leaves; and be sure to give him a gift when he marries.' Then he continued, 'You are not poor; why did you do that? Someone came to your house, and you sent him away.' In fact, a neighbor had come to request that we baptize her child. 'Father, I have five children, and it is difficult for me,' I told him. 'No, your error is elsewhere,' he replied. I had refused because I knew the neighbor was a very abrupt man, and I was afraid that after we were bound by the religious bonds of Baptism and became *koumbaroi*, we would have misunderstandings between us on account of the children. He could see far into the distant future."

He did not receive money for any religious services offered to the people. He gave strict penances to those who made oaths and who condemned people. He could see into the hearts of people as if they were an open book. Before his visitors told him their thoughts, he was able to know them and relate them precisely himself. He always spoke about love, humility, patience, repentance, charity, and forgiveness. Whatever he related about future events, they came to be as he had described them. To prevent people from honoring and praising him, he would send the sick on various sacred pilgrimages where they would invariably be healed. All remember him with great gratitude. The many circumstances in the life of this elder that reveal his gift of foresight create a sense of astonishment and amazement.

Whenever he celebrated the Divine Liturgy, he was transformed into another person. Pious worshippers would hear various sounds in the holy altar made by his heavenly visitors. They would bow down and whisper the "Lord, have mercy!" Once the saintly elder told his chanter, "Today I had so many saints, there was no place to put them! We had to place St. Panteleimon off in the corner; there was no space!" Once the demons were disturbing the elder and were not allowing him to offer the service of Proskomide. After the Liturgy he said, "I began this series of forty Liturgies with a great deal of pressure. The demons were shouting the names so loudly that I could not commemorate them and thus be forgiven." At another time after a series of forty Liturgies, someone asked him, "Geronda, did you weary yourself celebrating the forty Liturgies?" "No, my son, it was so delightful for me; it seemed like a single Vespers service, because they were very good people. Your father offered an abundant table laden with food, like Abraham did." Then the inquirer thought to himself, "We are really poor, on the verge of hunger; how did my father find a way to offer an abundant dinner?" "Don't look at it like that, my son," the elder corrected him. "Maybe he did not have anything to give, but his soul desired to give much, and so God measured it as if he were actually giving it." And he continued his remarks: "Your mother has acted like a dissatisfied employee toward your father, for she was somewhat tiresome and troublesome to him by always complaining. But your father stood firmly and always spoke to her with a gentle smile and kindness. Now, among your relatives you also have a blind woman, whose name you had forgotten to write. She is chaste and a very good person." But the man asked again, "How do you know her?" "When I commemorate the names over the *kollyva*, she comes also, but as visitor, a guest; she does not join the others. Now each one has taken his rightful place, and the way is now opened for you."

On another occasion, when a woman complained that he was reading the Gospel in Greek, he answered her, "Why are you complaining? Even if you did understand it, would you have done any of the things it says?" Those who knew him would often declare, "He could read clearly even our innermost thoughts and our most hidden sins." If you forgot to mention something in your confession, he would say, "Take a little stroll and you will remember something more." To one young lady he said, "Do you eat from an unwashed plate? No, of course not; you first wash it carefully with soap and make it clean, and then you eat your food from it. Well, that is just how it is with Christ; He wants your soul to be clean before He will come to dwell there!"

People would say about him, "We had a saint among us; it is too bad we did not have him a little longer." But he could see the sins of the people and was hoping to die, for he could not endure the evil and the sins of the world. The struggle that this man of God carried out was kept in secret very carefully. He was never seen eating normally, a full and hearty meal; he would simply eat a few pickled vegetables. He willingly deprived himself, for the great love of God. During the last forty days of his life, he barely ate anything. He ate some small, bitter wild pears, just to moisten his mouth.

He knew how to console, to lead to repentance and to sincere contrition. He had great compassion for every person. He would light candles for those who did not have anyone to remember them. He offered the Holy Unction and the Blessing of the Water for unknown people and for those who could not offer anything in return. He had abandoned himself and lived for others. Once some people had brought him a role of fabric as a gift. He gave it to one of his spiritual daughters to give to a widowed mother of four orphaned children. Upon receiving the gift, the family's joy was indescribable. Pascha was approaching, and they had no other means to provide some clothing for the orphans. The widow repeated again and again, "May that holy man be well, he who never forgets me!" When that spiritual daughter returned to the elder, she noticed that his face was shining with joy. He delighted in being able to help those in need. He encouraged people to baptize children in poor families, because their souls would find great benefit from that. It is said that the number of amazing things in the life of the elder was indeed great. May we understand that they were his gifts to us all whom he so loved and served sacrificially.

He was strenuously opposed to all types of sorcery. As long as there are such sorcerers, the people who go to them will undergo much suffering. He invited a woman who used to remove the spell of the evil eye and told her, "Come, tell me what you say, and I will teach you two prayers that will virtually make you a doctor!" He opened the book of the Horologion and found the *apolytikion* hymns of St. Haralampos and St. Blaise. From that time, with these two *apolytikia* and the prayers of the elder, not only people, but even animals, were healed.

Once he had gone to Drama to visit a family well known to him, and that night he received a visitation from St. George the Great Martyr, for whom he had particular reverence. The family offering hospitality to the elder was truly amazed by the event. They heard the martyr's dismounting in the yard and his ascent up to the elder's room. When asked about this in the morning, the elder told them everything. On another occasion the elder was in the same house, shut in without any sign of life for three days. On the third day he came out and told the man who offered him hospitality exactly what he was thinking. (The man had been troubled and wanted to call the police.) Then, with simplicity and emotion, the elder told him, "My son, the angels took me and for three days were carrying me around the heavens." And the reporter of this story concluded, "Both the life and the end of this humble monk, our elder, were sanctified. He showed us the way of virtue and left us with so many blessings and counsels, so that we too could follow this blessed way, if we so choose."

When a young lady, who later became Abbess Akylina, would go to Elder George, he would call her Mother Erasmia. The other older ladies would complain. He called her Mother Erasmia because he foreknew that she would become the abbess of his little monastery. People again said of him, "That elder of ours knew everything; he got into a person's soul. In everything he was a saint, and this is why we loved and appreciated him so much. He was so loving; you felt like he was your own father." Others have said, "Our entire family has benefited from the love and the prayers of this loving and sanctified elder of Sipsas. He used to tell us many things, but, as they say, the saint who is nearby receives no glory. We did not know his true significance. He was a living saint; whatever he told us—everything turned out to be true."

One Wednesday he went to a house near the monastery, and from the window asked the lady of the house, "What are you doing in there?" "I am eating with the children," came the answer. "What are you eating?" "We are drinking milk." "Maybe the small children can drink their milk, but you have no reason not to observe the Wednesday fast," he advised her in a fatherly yet rather stern manner. In the neighboring town in those days, everyone was fasting except for the infants. Only two or three persons in the village did not keep the fast. He knew them but said nothing to them. This is God's way; if you want, you are free to follow it. Everyone listened to him because they loved him. When he passed by the school, all the children, about a hundred, would line up to kiss his hand. He also inspired their teacher in a spiritual way.

The holy elder attended all the funerals. His presence alone was enough to console the grieving families, but his words were even more consoling. He himself would go to visit the sick and to console them. He deprived himself to give to others. At that time there was much poverty in the villages. Everyone wore mended clothes. Even the elder wore a mended cassock and apron. He never remained idle; he was always doing something.

During the Supplications and the Vespers, he would invite the children to come and chant, to learn the hymn "O Virgin Theotokos" and other hymns. "Then," as the children have reported, "the divine grace would sometimes come, and one could see him not walking on the ground. He spoke another language, chanting in Georgian, but what he said then was another, heavenly language." He was teaching the children from an early age to stand quietly during the sacred services. He wanted them to be connected with divine worship early on. Sometimes when he was reading the Holy Gospel from the royal gate, they could see that he was not stepping on the floor. Beyond the reports of marvelous and exceptional events in the life of the elder, what impressed me most were the expressions of love of his spiritual children, who, I believe, were not merely being sentimental but were recognizing and authentically expressing his holiness.

This is the sort of thing they say: "I would come, bow, kiss his hand, and he would always strike me on the shoulder. He was not a man like us; he was a saint. On Christmas and Pascha I would always go to be blessed, to receive his blessing . . . I confess that only if one is a saint does he not stop at the human, trite, and worldly things, but goes on to embrace all of us as his sheep, and he as our shepherd. Yes, he was indeed for all of us a shepherd and father." Another person has reported, "He taught us to have respect for our elders, patience in deprivations and poverty, and to know the power of prayer, the blessings of charitable benevolence, and the evil of blasphemy and obscene language."

His austerity was due to a sense of righteousness and love; he aimed to teach and to benefit the people. Once a woman who visited the sorcerers went to visit the elder. He did not even allow her to enter into the courtyard. "From a distance!" he shouted when she complained. "Listen to me from a distance, and when you have given up all the things you do and you change your way of life, then you can come to me. I do not do sorcery. I will accept you only when you have repented and have come to my faith." Later he explained himself further to the niece of that woman: "My child, go and tell that aunt of yours to change her ways with all those things she is doing, to come in repentance to my way, and then she will be always welcome. Fire comes, my child, and burns everything where it comes; it does not burn only one, but all of us." The young niece also correctly observed, "With the luminous eyes of his soul, he could see the blazing evil of the demons coming against us."

Moreover, his spiritual children would say, "In our every step into daily life, we had an illumined elder, who corrected our mistakes and our sins and reminded us what the holy will of God is, so that we should never forget. He taught us many things, and we owe him much." The town of Sipsas was truly blessed as long as the holy elder was alive. If two persons were at odds over something, the elder would send the children to these persons and tell them to go and see the elder, who was expecting them. He in turn would reconcile them immediately in the spiritual way that he knew and practiced so well. He knew everybody, and he prayed for everyone. If someone did not make it to church one Sunday, by the next Sunday he had sent him a message to find out what had caused him to not come to church. He never allowed neighbors to be at odds with one another; he reconciled them directly.

The earthly end of the saintly father George was truly blessed. He had felt it coming; he had foreseen and foretold it long before. He awaited death with thanksgiving, praise, and joy. He gave instructions on exactly how he wanted to be buried with his clerical vestments and liturgical books. He alerted all of his spiritual children so he could bless them and to bid them farewell. He departed from this life with psalms and hymns and tears. He celebrated his final Divine Liturgy and later made his final confession to Pappa Stavros. The mystery of Holy Unction was also offered. Thousands of people were at the funeral, and the two cypress trees there bowed in reverence, while thousands of birds covered the sky. His last words were "Open to me the gates of compassion, O blessed Theotokos . . ." He reposed in the Lord on November 4, 1959. Fifty years later, his memory remains alive.

One insignificant, obscure, oppressed, harassed, sickly, and disabled person with very little education attracted abundantly the grace of God. His great love for God and man, his humility, and his charitable works made him pleasing before God. This is holiness according to God's will.

After his death the saint revealed himself in various ways to many, in order to console them, to strengthen them, and support them. People observed a light at his grave, breathed in a fragrance in his cell, and felt his presence in his church. He would also visit the sick to heal and help them in their need.

On February 2, 2006, after a fervent request by all the nuns of the Convent of the Ascension, with the blessing of the blessed abbess Akylina and with the official order of the local metropolitan, the most-reverend Paul, the sacred relics of the elder were transferred. Their color was a coffee-yellow, and they were fragrant, while on his skull there was a paradoxically fashioned sign of the cross. With the initiative of the same saint-loving metropolitan, all the necessary preparations were enacted for the canonical recognition of his sanctity.

Before concluding this humble presentation, I want to include the narrative of a young man who made a particularly good impression on me when he came some years ago to the annual commemoration of the saint at his monastery (which, by the way, is flourishing today by his prayers):

> I remember that it was cold, but we had not yet entered the room where the people had been gathered. We had sat next to the spot where the elder was buried. The people were lighting candles. At one point a woman of about sixty years came, lit candles, and reverenced the tomb. Since we had not yet entered to hear what they were saying, I asked her if she knew the elder. She then began to relate her acquaintance with the elder. She lived in Drama and had often gone to church in the monastery of the elder. After the Liturgy one day, he told her, "You run to doctors and spend your money to no avail. Your child will be healed by the great physician," he said, and pointed to heaven. He told her that the entire family should keep a forty-day fast and then come to receive Holy Communion at the monastery. And this is what happened. The child was healed completely after receiving Holy Communion, and since then has been most healthy and without any problems at all. When I told her something about the elder as a person from the past, she replied, "The elder has not left us. He is here. He is beside us. He helps us. I beseech him at every circumstance in my life."
>
> The woman related other events after the death of the elder. She said that he appeared in a room where she was sitting with other women. He entered while the doors were shut. He gave them advice about their journey in life. I was really surprised by this uneducated woman and by all the things she related so simply and naturally, without a trace of pride. She did not have the attitude of a person relating

things of such spiritual height, but was deeply joyful and simply trying to say, "Look at who I am and what I have been blessed to experience!"

On the ninth day after the death of the elder, the weather was bad, and this woman and a friend of hers were in the elder's cell. Late at night they went to where the elder was buried to see if the vigil lamp had gone out. From the grave a thick white light was coming out and was rising up high. Both women were able to see it and felt reassured that this was a sanctifying and very beneficial light. They reached out as if to take some with their hands and applied it on their heads and faces, for they were suffering from headaches. The other woman also applied this light to her stomach, which was hurting. From that moment their illnesses were healed.

We, as students, preoccupied with books and theological themes, were entirely unfamiliar with the essence and the experience of such conditions, and this left us speechless. In any case, the spiritual maturity of this uneducated woman and the proof of her healthy ecclesial mentality was demonstrated by what she told me at one point as we stood there and talked for over an hour. By seeing, perhaps, our youth and our miserable condition, she told us, "I feel very sorry for the young people and for the way they are living; they will not be able to have joy in their life. They are being tormented by the things they are doing. Every day on my knees I beseech the all-holy Theotokos to protect and guard and enlighten the young people in finding joy in their life." Hers was a very different approach from the usual accusations leveled irresponsibly by every "pious" person against the truly tormenting lifestyle of the youth then and now, and perhaps this is why it made a strong impression in my mind.

In any case, independently of this conversation, there was something that drew us to this place, and we would come often, whenever we had an opportunity. I remember the blessed Abbess Akylina, who always offered us hospitality and fed us in a small room. I do not remember what she said to us, but I do remember that she was always full of light and joy. From the various conversations, from the things I heard and especially from the atmosphere of the area and the feelings that were evoked by the church and the tomb of Elder George, I had the feeling that this was a great saint of our Church. I also remember that even on Mt. Athos, where I talked to the monks there about this elder, they told me that this man had the greatest gift of foresight in recent times.

His holiness has finally come to be honored officially by our Church, and we can now call upon him, even as before, but now we also do it to honor him officially, as he so deserves. May we have his blessing and his protection, and may we be at least worthy to call upon him in prayer.

To this I have nothing to add. I simply countersign the beautiful and appropriate words of this young man, as related above. The pure holiness of the saint, the guileless spirituality of his spiritual children, and even the spirituality of those who did not know him affect us, indeed, most profoundly and should raise our spiritual awareness in a very beneficial way.

3

FOOLS FOR CHRIST

ST. ANTHONY SAID THAT A TIME WILL COME when the insane people will call the rational people crazy, because they are not the same as themselves. It appears that he was speaking about our time. Today someone is a fornicator, and people call him a free man; he is an adulterer, and they call him a daring hero; a thief, and people say he is smart and cunning. On the other hand, a young man practices self-control and is considered to be a simpleton; a hard-working man who is honest and honorable is thought to be foolish; a modest young lady is considered to be old-fashioned. An educated young man who goes to become a monk on Mt. Athos or somewhere else is looked upon with an ironic and jeering smile. The people of the world will confront with reservation, suspicion, and rejection those who are struggling to maintain a degree of sincerity, prudence, reverence, and spiritual contrition in their life. The majority considers such people extremists and will readily marginalize them. Those who today observe faithfully the gospel are considered by most to be foolish, while the more genteel among the many will, at least, accept the pious condescendingly.

To be a true Christian today will require a cost, a risk; it is an adventure, a confession, a form of "foolishness." To be a Christian is not for the indolent, the self-centered, the idle, the superficial, and the fearful. The Christian today must be intelligent, enthusiastic, courageous, daring, and fearless. The saints of our Church who were fools for Christ inspire and guide us into this transcendence, helping us to move outside of our shell of individualism and the frozen ego and to enter into the realm of spiritual health and balance, which is marked by a holy humility.

The Greek word σαλός means one who is troubled, unbalanced, crazy. It also means an imbecile, an idiot, someone who is foolish and ridiculous because he has a small or even a great psychic or pathological problem. Not all of these types of people are the same, and not all are ready to be committed to a psychiatric hospital or to take handfuls of psychiatric drugs, just so that they might not be any trouble to us. Some of these people may have a head injury, which may or may not be correctable, whereas others may have come to where they are through inordinate egotism and much pride. Still others may have been affected by great grief and worry, while still others may be affected by a hypersensitivity that does not allow them to live comfortably in this unstable, harsh, and violent world.

The blessed elder Paisios the Haghiorite used to tell us that a young man who had serious psychological problems once visited him in his cell. During his first visit, we were told, the young man sat with the elder for eight hours. The elder did not even move his legs, so that the young man would not imagine that he was tiring the elder. The elder listened carefully and only spoke occasionally. This was the first time in his life that this young man had spoken so comfortably. Everyone before had criticized him abruptly: "You fool! You don't know what you're talking about! Stop! You have no idea what's going on!" When the young man finished, the elder told him, "My young man, instead of going to be treated with those electric shocks, why don't you come here to me?" When I asked the elder, out of curiosity, what he did for the young man, he answered me with a monastic expression: "I comforted his thinking. His mind was being twisted out of shape by obsessive thoughts that his family did not love him and that people hated him." After this the young man went to the elder from time to time and grew better and better. During the last time, his father accompanied him, bringing also a letter from his mother. The mother had written in the letter something that the father also apparently agreed with: "Father Paisios, our child loves you, he appreciates you, and he listens to you. Please tell him that when we have guests at home for a celebration, he should not make an appearance and embarrass us before our guests. Tell him also, please, not to go to his father's place of work"—he was the director of a bank—"because, again, he embarrasses him in front of the employees." Then the young man got up and said to his father before Elder Paisios, "Can't you humble yourself and accept that you have a sick child, and that if you endure this, you will even have a reward in heaven?" And the elder remarked to me, "Tell me, who is the sick person? Is it the one presumed to have a psychological problem, or the parents who presume to be knowledgeable? Seeing the child with certain difficulties, why do you force him to put both feet into one shoe? Is this not the case?" In the final analysis, the question is the same: Who is really crazy, and who is rational?

Today it is easy to characterize as crazy a young man who speeds down the road on a motorcycle, who wears strange clothes and haircuts, who spends his nights in nightclubs and wanders about as a vagrant. Have we sat down to talk with him as a loving father, to see why he reacts negatively and why he provokes us and shouts? A problematic young person harms only himself by his prodigality, by using alcohol and drugs. Maybe it is time to see with greater understanding, forbearance, and tolerance all of these young people of ours who are troubled, and who in their heart are not really vagrants, and we certainly cannot just simply call them crazy and thus be exonerated of any responsibility for them.

Sometimes a person will be led into psychological madness to avoid constant worries and vexations that trouble him all the more when he is compelled to think rationally. As a result, he goes about in untidy clothes; carelessly; without shame, fear, or any pretension. In a sense he is free and happy. When there is no conscience, there is no accountability, and one can live in a constant simplistic blessedness. A crazy person is abhorrent, undesirable, easily rejected and excluded. No society ever wanted to have crazy people as equal members. Rational thought never permitted such a concession. On the contrary, these powerless, defenseless, and hurt people were persecuted, ridiculed, distressed, stoned, despised in the worst way, abused most vulgarly, and sometimes even put to death. For them there was no dignity, honor, or pleasure. But how much dignity existed among their wise and honorable persecutors?

Elder Aimilianos of Simonos Petra, with his knowledge and wisdom, explained how the fools for Christ had, in fact, a degree of craziness. The fool for Christ represents the most difficult form of holiness: a virtuous, wise, and charismatic person pretends to be a fool, in order to be in a state of constant humility. We who are indeed sinful, unwise, and at fault become greatly angered when people make a justifiable remark at our expense. Think of the reserve of divine power and the degree of humility that these genuine men of God had . . .

My brothers and sisters, a fool for Christ, with his pretended foolishness, is really struggling to rouse his rational fellow human beings to take their life seriously, to understand why they are living, and to see the purpose of their existence. Thus, his whole stance, his movements and actions, is intended to awaken consciences from the lethargy of sinfulness and to lead them to correction, to regret, to repentance. This history begins from the time of the prophets of the Old Testament, who were received with great reservation by the people, whose sins and transgressions were being censured.

A contemporary scholar, Ikaros Petrides, writes most appropriately, "We encounter the Prophet Ezekiel, for example, eating bread that has been kneaded with the dung of animals, in order to show how sin had spread throughout Jerusalem. We see the Prophet Jeremiah wearing a yoke around his neck, like the yoke placed over animals, to demonstrate the imminent captivity of the Israelites. The Prophet Hosea, who wanted to represent the infidelity of his countrymen, himself lived with a prostitute. The Prophet Isaiah, who foretold the captivity of his people to the Egyptians and the Assyrians, walked around for three years without clothes and without sandals on his feet." Any such similarly strange behavior will certainly startle, scandalize, and provoke, but there is always a profound reason and a significant purpose, which the saints of all ages uphold in advance in order to lead the faithful to an awakening, an inspiration, a consolation, a respite, a repentance. The foolishness of the saints certainly served as an alarm to awaken the people.

This foolishness for Christ, with its labor, its pain, and its difficulty, was meant to liberate people and to offer them spiritual health in various ways. The saints who were fools for Christ were able in a myriad of ways to censure deeds, to purge transgressions, and thus to create opportunities for the correction of souls. The saints themselves, with their pretended foolishness, which is known only to their spiritual father, concealed their virtues. The divine virtues had been acquired in advance, before they entered the way of foolishness for Christ. Thus they were well prepared and armed to confront great temptations. They themselves had first been sufficiently helped and were thus able to help others. This is how the spiritual law functions; there is no other way.

The behavior of those who feign foolishness for the sake of Christ is strange and rationally inexplicable, and it provokes scandal in those who are presumably pious and moral. The life of these holy fools is not ordered within the realm of an organized Christian community. Even the Church attempted to limit the phenomenon by stating in a decision of the Sixth Ecumenical Council that such persons must not pretend to be possessed by the devil, nor feign depravity and act out their antics. However, the revelation of their godly life, their mystical teaching, and their guidance of many to repentance convinced the Church to recognize them and to appropriately name them fools for Christ.

The holy fools for Christ chose a narrow way, an uphill way that is difficult, wearisome, burdensome, and daring. Hiding their virtue well, they willed to help others in a very peculiar manner. It required great dexterity, art, and science to constantly hide their virtuous life and to always present themselves as the opposite of what they really were. The main purpose of their foolishness was the deliberate and persistent concealment of their known virtue. This martyrdom made them all the more humble. Through the irony, the shame, the ridicule, the persecutions, and tribulations, they were cleansed, illumined, and sanctified, and thus acquired genuine and resplendent humility. The fool for Christ made fun of the deceit, the wretchedness, the vagueness, and the insincerity of the people, even while these censured people were ridiculing them. The fools for Christ knew their limits, how far to go and how much to censure. According to St. John of Sinai, the author of the *Ladder of Divine Ascent*, a great amount of discretion is needed in this particular struggle, so that the demons, whom we seek to mock, will not in fact mock us.

These blessed and courageous saints became lawless, idiotic, dishonorable, and foolish men for the sake of Christ, as St. Paul says in his First Letter to the Corinthians. They made the impossible possible in order to please Almighty God. They possessed, so to speak, an irrational logic, which seems incomprehensible to us apparently serious, pious, moral, proper, impatient, and unwearied people. They died to be raised up, even before their biological death. They were not imbeciles, naïve, or miserable. They did not have poverty of spirit, which the Lord blessed, but they did acquire it through their bloody struggle. God motivated some of these extraordinary saints so that they could help other souls with their unusual way of life.

St. Andrew the Fool for Christ received from the Lord Himself the exhortation to become a fool for His sake. With the blessing of his spiritual father, Nikephoros, who was a parish priest in the great church of St. Sophia in Constantinople in the fifth century, he followed this difficult way toward holiness. He was not terrified by the severe warfare against him by the demons and the people. People took him to be in fact crazy and possessed by demons. Through his prayer he was informed that this way of life was indeed God's will for him. He found great consolation in the divine visions that sweetened his bitter life. All day long he endured the mockery, the ridicule, the abuse, and the cursing of the mindless people. They entertained themselves at the expense of a saint. He endured all the abuse without complaint. He even played the role of a jester to please the crowds. But he dedicated all his nights to the Lord, with fervent prayers and many tears. He spent the night with the homeless people and the dogs of the streets. He prayed to the Lord to forgive the sins of those who harmed and embittered him during the day, and to place their sins upon his soul. One day some prostitutes pushed him into their house. In various ways they provoked him to sin with them. The only thing that the blessed man did was to laugh very loudly, thus mocking the deceptive demon of fornication itself. In the coldness of winter, when many died from exposure to the cold, he experienced the beauty of the warmth of paradise and did not suffer any harm. When someone saw him making the sign of the cross and causing the doors of the church to open and again to close, this person marveled and said, "Look at the person called an irrational fool by those who are really the fools!" With many marvelous signs and with foreknowledge of his death, St. Andrew the Fool for Christ reposed in a most blessed way.

St. Maximos Kausokalivites, after receiving a directive from the all-holy Theotokos, went to the summit of Mt. Athos, where he received heavenly bread and was again directed by her to live alone in the ravines of the mountain, because in this way he would become the cause of salvation for many. He lived many years with great deprivations, without giving his flesh the slightest ease, wandering barefoot throughout the wild regions and abandoning himself to the severe cold of winter and the heat of summer. As he moved from place to place, he would also burn his huts, so that he might not be tied to anything material and earthy. He rejoiced in being mocked and derided rather than in being honored and respected. Within his incoherent uttering, if you persisted and paid attention, you could find wise counsels and teachings. When St. Gregory of Sinai encountered him and was informed of his achievements, he suggested that he live simply in one place, because many were in need of him. St. Maximos obeyed the directive and helped many to rid themselves of the foolishness of sinfulness. He was an important ascetic of Mt. Athos in the fourteenth century.

The Lord indicated to St. Andrew this way of life, as He did also with St. Symeon the Fool for Christ, whereas the all-holy Theotokos, the protector of the Holy Mountain, directed St. Maximos. Other saints assumed this uphill way on their own in order to be saved themselves and to save others. It is also a fact that the following of this foolish way of life was not always only for the purpose of saving others. The great love for Christ was the primary reason. This extraordinary love moved the saints to abandon wealth, honors, prominence, relatives, friends, countries—everything. They chose to live poorly, in deprivation, without glory and honor, despised by people, and with many difficulties. For the wise intellectuals, the clever, knowledgeable, and learned people, this departure from the world was considered to be a great madness and a deception. God, however, desires all of our love, for He is a jealous God. The love for God is supreme and above all things. It is from this ultimate love that all the other loves emanate.

Today if a young man or woman goes to a monastery, this young person is considered to have something wrong with him; he is thought to not be well. Such a departure is usually confronted with suspicion and reservation. Even those living in the world and struggling to observe the evangelical virtues are looked upon curiously as extremists, strange, peculiar, backward, and marginalized. My brothers and sisters, it is certainly far more preferable for us to be ridiculed by our fellow human beings than for us to be weeping eternally.

Even Christ Himself was badly misunderstood, misinterpreted, and crucified. The stance, words, and actions of Christ troubled the hypocritical Pharisees. Christ exposed them, and they could not endure this at all. Christ unmasked them, and their pride could not in the least stand it. These contemporaries of Christ, with their great intelligence, were greatly scandalized by Him. Why did He work miracles of healing on the Sabbath, which was the day of rest? Why did He sit at the same table to eat in the homes of sinful and miserable tax collectors? How could He allow the sinful woman to wash His feet? How could He dare to promise paradise to women who were prostitutes? They considered Jesus, who expelled the demons, to be possessed by demons; the one who was wise to be foolish; even his relatives considered Him to be "beside Himself" and not well, according to St. Mark (3:21). This is how he was mocked, scoffed, spat upon, struck, sent away, dishonored, and crucified by the leaders of Judaism.

We could say, my brothers and sisters, that the apostles experienced the same fate. The Apostle Paul says to the Corinthians very characteristically,

> For I think that God has displayed us, the apostles, last, as men condemned to death; for we have been made a spectacle to the world, both to angels and to men. We are fools for Christ's sake, but you are wise in Christ! We are weak, but you are strong! You are distinguished, but we are dishonored! To the present hour we both hunger and thirst, and we are poorly clothed, and beaten, and homeless. And we labor, working with our own hands. Being reviled, we bless; being persecuted, we endure; being defamed, we entreat. We have been made as the filth of the world, the offscouring of all things until now. (1 Cor 4:9–13)

The Evangelist Matthew records that even the Lord Himself has said that those who are shamed and persecuted for His sake will be blessed: "Blessed are you when they revile and persecute you, and say all kinds of evil against you falsely for My sake. Rejoice and be exceedingly glad, for great is your reward in heaven, for so they persecuted the prophets who were before you" (5:11–12). We could say then that the life of the fools for Christ is based upon these words of Sacred Scripture.

In studying the amazing, engaging, and emotional lives of these saints, these fools for Christ, we must observe that what they have in common is their great love for God; their desire to help their neighbor; and their asceticism, which goes beyond measure. Most of them lived in Russia during the past two centuries. There are about one hundred, men and women, and we meet them in the virgin forests, in the busy streets of Moscow or St. Petersburg, naked or half-naked, barefoot, unwashed, uncombed, in rags, homeless, hungry, persecuted, troubled, and so extraordinarily peculiar that they are seen by the people as crazy vagrants. They in fact perform miracles, teach, correct, and guide many to repentance and to the revelation of the hidden things of their heart.

St. Pelagia Ivanova (+1884) chose from an early age to feign foolishness for the sake of Christ by doing various irrational things. Everyone scolded her for this, and very few suspected her hidden inner work. As she grew up she became a beautiful young lady, and, in spite of her peculiarities, many requested to marry her. At the age of nineteen, she married a harsh man. Her encounter with St. Seraphim of Sarov confirmed the authenticity of her difficult struggle. For entire nights she kept a vigil in the yard of her house or of the church in her town, without concern for the cold. If someone praised her, she increased her bizarre behavior. Ironic laughter became a permanent companion of her life but never subdued her. Because of her irrational behavior, her husband would often beat her, and yet she had three children with him. She would even go begging in order to be humbled all the more. Whatever she gathered from begging she distributed to the poor and to the churches. Many times after a severe beating, she would bleed and collapse as if coming close to death. Out of her irrational words, the gift of foresight was often abundantly revealed. She ended up in convent, where even there very few nuns detected her well-hidden virtue. She in turn did not cease her provocations. She would break the glass windows of the cells, probe into the piles of dung, wash with unclean water, and carry large stones, bricks, and lumber. She kept hidden a golden heart through patience, humility, faith, and prayer. Toward the end of her life, her hidden virtue began to be revealed, even though this was not her will. Her prophetic words came true. This apparently foolish and mindless woman surpassed the many rational people of her time and place.

A similar life was lived by St. Matrona (+1911), who was widowed, and instead of continuing to serve as a nurse, she decided to distribute all her possessions to the poor and to courageously follow the way of foolishness for Christ. She wandered barefoot all year to the various sacred places of pilgrimage as a humble pilgrim, wearing poor white clothing. She always traveled by foot. She went on a pilgrimage to Jerusalem four times. During the final thirty years of her life, she was in St. Petersburg. To prevent people from honoring her, even though her prayer caused miracles to happen, she did not cease doing various foolish things. Whatever was given to her, she distributed directly to the poor, who truly loved her very much for this. Thousands of people approached her to be helped. Many alcoholics found healing in her presence. At her funeral, which she foresaw and foretold, there were twenty-five thousand people, many of whom had been assisted by her in various ways. St. Matrona performs miracles to this day.

St. Barnabas the Bishop (+1963) learned piety and reverence from his virtuous mother. From a young age he desired to become a monk and became acquainted with important elders (startsi) of pre-revolutionary Russia. He excelled in all of his studies. He was persecuted and imprisoned by the atheistic regime. He observed with his own eyes the execution of holy hierarchs of the Church. In 1920 he was ordained bishop and had his see at the Lavra of the Kiev Caves. The monks there observed in his behavior a certain strangeness that was inexplicable for them. When he was exiled for criticizing the serious mistakes of an archbishop, he was very joyful, because he now had sufficient time for prayer. He too decided to follow the narrow way of foolishness for the sake of Christ. Day and night he would shed tears in prayer over the sins of the Russian people, who denied God and were now suffering under the Soviet regime. While all others were afraid to admit that they were Christians, he boldly and fearlessly confessed it. He even managed to obtain a paper stating that he was mentally deranged. He thus moved about easily now as an officially declared crazy person. He went about in an overcoat with a tattered cassock underneath, with his beard shaven and his hair cut. For a period of time he had been hiding in the house of a friend, praying and writing. When he was finally imprisoned, he took advantage of the occasion and taught those in prison. He was later released from prison and endured other tribulations. Once when they went to seize him and imprison him again, he was very seriously ill and could not be moved. When he became better, he went on his own to surrender himself to the authorities. He was sentenced to three years in a concentration camp in Siberia. He was placed first with the criminals who had heavy penalties and later in the psychiatric ward, where he lived a horrible hell, being beaten and abused by the really mentally ill inmates. He, nevertheless, lived in paradise by praying for, forgiving, and blessing everyone. Many knew of his gift of foresight and the hidden wisdom of his words. During his funeral the face of this "crazy" bishop shone with an extraordinary light.

Even in Greece we have such saints and virtuous elders.

The saintly Gervasios Karakalinos (+1830) from Gomati in Chalkidike went to the Holy Mountain as a young man and became a monk in the Monastery of Karakalou. After a long ascetic period in the monastery, he decided to continue his asceticism alone and chose the way of holiness we are now discussing. He wandered all around the Holy Mountain in his peculiar way and provoked the people who did not know him to mock and ridicule him on account of his odd manner of life. When after his death his sacred relics exuded a sweet fragrance, this enabled all to understand the correctness of his peculiar ascetic way of life toward holiness.

The saintly Anthimos the Haghiorite (+1867) came from Bulgaria. After the death of his presbytera, he went to the Holy Mountain and lived as a monk in the Monasteries of Simonos Petra, St. Panteleimon, and Zographou. Most of the time, however, he spent in the desert areas, the forests, the caves, and the hollows of large trees. He wore a large burlap bag as a cassock. With his foolish behavior, he was able to carefully conceal his virtue. He fasted alone and many times remained completely without food. Whenever he ate with others, he made it a point to eat in a gluttonous manner. Very few people knew of his gift of foresight. He avoided honors as diligently as others seek after them.

Elder Filaretos of the Karoulia (+1962) came from the Rysio area of Constantinople and as a young man went to the Monastery of Stavroniketa, where he lived as a monk for twelve years, after which he went to the fearsome Karoulia to live as an ascetic hermit. Pretending to be a mindless fool, he gave up his responsibility of directing the monastery. He departed for the Karoulia, and there he considered his humble and poor hut to be a palace. He gladly shared the meager produce of his tiny garden with his fellow ascetic hermits. His usual food consisted of old dried bread with boiled green vegetables mixed with ground bran. He went about barefoot, clothed in rags, completely without possessions, sleeping always on the ground with only a log for a pillow. He realized that he would soon die and prepared his grave. He called upon the Danielite Fathers to come and chant his beloved hymn "It Is Truly Right" (Ἄξιόν ἐστιν) for the last time, and then on the very next day the one who was truly "a lover of virtue" fell asleep in the Lord in a truly peaceful and blessed death.

The Romanian elder Herodion (+1990) also went to the Holy Mountain as a young man and lived the monastic life in various places. He ended up in the desert area of Kapsala, where many virtuous and saintly fathers had lived. He lived very poorly, completely deprived, without any ease or comfort. His cell reminded one of a very dirty and unkept storage area. The disorder and uncleanliness of his cell concealed a clean and peaceful heart. His unintelligible and incoherent words concealed his wisdom, which censured those who may speak nicely but who are without life experiences consistent with this speech. Those who were virtuous were able to understand him well. The others considered him to be a Godforsaken fool, and this pleased him. Whatever food supplies were brought to him he threw away. He lived without any heat in the cold winters. For his cassock he wore a torn military blanket. This is how I encountered him one afternoon outside of his cell, wearing a child-like smile.

One can easily be puzzled and ask, "What is the meaning of all these things for the contemporary worldly man? Are they prototypes for imitation?" We are not saying this at all. This kind of holy foolishness cannot touch any rationally thinking person. An extreme amount of rationality can become another type of irrationality. Today the irrationalities of the people are different. We are not talking about imitating these kinds of saints.

Foolishness for the sake of Christ is a particular grace and gift of the Holy Spirit. It is given to the few and elect. The fools for Christ, with their sublime achievements and their unimaginable spiritual acrobatics, teach the proud and unhumbled people of our contemporary times what humility is. They are contrite and want to bring compunction to the egotistic heart, which is hard like a rock. With their heavenly flights, they want to raise us up a little from earthly things and concerns. The supernatural and superrational conditions of their divine life should not only simply excite and enthuse us but also censure us in a creative and fertile way, so that we might become more humbly prudent.

In our irrational times, when unbalanced ideas prevail, we have constant conflicts, different battles, and great wars. Usually people blame only the others and place upon them the burden of responsibility, and they do this with considerable superficiality and pride. Many say that if they held the power in their hands, they would directly put order to the world, despite the fact that they have not yet succeeded in making peace with a neighbor, their husband or wife, or even with themselves. The first war was between the devil and God. From that time the devil wars against the people of God and attempts, if possible, to mislead even the elect. He of course does not always succeed. God has not allowed him to have unlimited power. Demonic traps and various temptations can become for the believer opportunities for maturity, refinement, and progress. Today every resistance to the demonic and worldly mentality is considered by the many, unfortunately, as being irrational and foolishness.

Christ said it in a timely fashion: that in this life we must be warriors, even within our own family; our own people will behave as enemies because we follow the Christian life. Real peace is to be found only in the meeting of man with God. By having this divine peace, we have everything and become fearless before every aggression and every enemy. By having the peace of God, we can then have true peace with our fellow human beings.

Christians today must understand well that their ethics, their criteria, and their mentality are all in opposition to the worldly ones. Worldly people in turn consider Christians to be out of touch with this world. They see us as peculiar, irrational, and foolish; backward and old-fashioned people worthy of every ironic remark, ridicule, and disdain. If these are the things that Christ Himself endured, as did the apostles and all the saints, why should we be excluded? The early Christians were considered to be crazy and were subjected to terrible martyrdoms by the pagans, who then worshipped idols. Even today the various neopagans are unable to understand that there are people who, for the sake of their faith and their principles, will renounce their interests, their rights, and their justification for the sake of a heavenly reward and for the eternal, most joyful kingdom of God. Prudent Christians are considered, by the worldly people of our times, as slow, mindless, backward, infantile, and foolish. In the final analysis, however, the foolish are those who do not believe in God. Sacred Scripture says, "The fool has said in his heart, 'There is no God'" (Ps 14:1; 53:1). Indeed, it is atheism that is foolishness. Imprudent foolishness is also greed, as the Gospel says in the Parable of the Rich Man: "Fool! This night your soul will be required of you" (Luke 12:20). Imprudent and foolish was also the young man in the evangelical narratives who preferred earthly and not heavenly treasures (see Matt 19:16–22; Mark 10:17–22; Luke 18:18–23). A rational person is one who exchanges the temporal for the eternal. Such a person is inspired not only by the fools for Christ but also by all the saints and by

Christ Himself—all of whom were considered to be fools by the irrational people of the world.

The fools for Christ did not want to be esteemed nor honored; they did not want to be praised and glorified. They preferred to be despised, criticized, mocked, and ridiculed. Who among us accepts such a thing? Who prays for his persecutors? Who loves his accusers? We who are considered to be rational and dignified cannot accept even a justifiable remark of criticism against us. The saints hated glory and preferred to be despised. The fools for Christ may not have been extremely ascetic fasters, vigil keepers, and great ascetics, but they had achieved a goal at the very center of Orthodox spiritual life, which is the holy humility that exalts and deifies. Like a powerful magnet, humility attracts the grace of God in abundance. Humility can be easily attained with self-debasement, self-denigration, and self-nullification, and by being aware of our nothingness. With their holy craziness these saints were able to conceal their virtue very effectively.

By wearing the heavy mantel of foolishness, they were able to protect themselves from dangerous praise and from precarious and uncertain honors. The holy martyrs who were fools for Christ played a heroic game. They mocked pride, vainglory, and greed for the worldly possessions of this vain and fallen world. They mocked hypocritical worldliness, silly airs of nobility, foolish vainglories, masquerading political intrigues, theatrical affectations and ostentations, and the pharisaical mentality of fallen and decadent religiosity. They wanted to contribute in alleviating in the world the spirit of a false and inauthentic dignity that hides great pride and egotism. In the final analysis, it is rather comical and laughable to hide in fear and terror from your real pain and to be concerned only about "what the people will say about us" or "how it isn't right that we appear like this to the world."

The demons experienced a great defeat in the persons of the truly humble fools for Christ, because the demons, above all, fear and tremble before holy humility. A fool for Christ in Russia used to stand in front of the churches to throw stones at their windows, and at the doors of the brothels, where he would kiss the steps in front of them. After his death his spiritual father revealed that he was throwing the stones because he could see the demons wanting to enter the church, and he kissed the steps of the brothels because he saw angels standing there and weeping.

The difficult way to holiness represented by the fools for Christ requires a divine calling and an abundance of grace, otherwise one will not be able to mock the world, but will be mocked by the world and the most cunning of demons. The Holy Spirit must kindle his heart so that he is able to endure all the abuse of the world in the same way as the apostles, who were considered by the ignorant people to be drunk. Otherwise it is not possible. Only one who loves God greatly can endure these conditions and remain firmly established in this sublime and difficult struggle. Abba Barsanoufios says that God does not like the things that men like. If the things that worldly people depreciate and devalue are done for God, these become praiseworthy and blessed when seen and judged by God.

Sophia, the great twentieth-century ascetic of the Monastery of Kleisoura in Kastoria, practiced foolishness for Christ, together with other difficult ascetic achievements, such as constant humility, love of poverty, and philanthropy. The holiness of her life was seen when her sacred relics exuded a sweet fragrance. People have spoken also about a certain "Crazy John" in Athens, who kept hidden, under his excesses and foolery, a golden heart that loved Christ and his fellow human beings. At his funeral the entire neighborhood that had experienced them spoke about his mystical interventions in their life and how he had corrected their errors and guided them in a changed way of life that led them toward salvation.

The various intellectuals of our time find it impossible to understand the condition of grace possessed by the fools for Christ. Even modern Christians have considerable difficulty in following this kind of holiness with ease. They are troubled, scandalized, and burdened with problematic questions. The fools for Christ will always exist as a protest to a cold and calculated rationalism, to an unhealthy and superficial moralistic exterior of proper and polite behavior. They also censure our superficial faith and our shallow trust in God. Our easy criticism and condemnation of the other is certainly restrained by these utterly humble saints.

May the saints, the friends of God and our own good friends, intercede always for all of us. We—all of us—have a great need for their ever-vigilant and powerful intercessions.

4

The New Martyrs of Chios

The beautiful island of Chios was named "the myrrh-bearing island" for its fragrant mastic, its great variety of flower-bearing trees, and its multicolored flowers. Its history is ancient, with a rich tradition of cultural accomplishments and a great offering upon the altar of freedom. Personally, I believe that this island is truly myrrh-bearing because it has offered a special fragrance to our country and the world through the beautiful and sacred personalities of heroes and saints who reflected a noble spirit and a way of life that our world always needs. Today we know by name at least fifty such saints, and the story of each of their lives exudes a spiritual fragrance.

Various conquerors have passed through Chios, seeking to change many things, including the faith of its noble inhabitants. Their resistance, however, was strong and tremendous. Certain times they countersigned their faith with their own blood. The teachers, the clergy, the monasteries, and the churches often served as a refuge for the persecuted people of the island. The resistance of these subjugated people was indeed courageous, heroic, and sacrificial, and became a source of courage and hope for the others and for those who came afterward. Their deeply rooted religious faith was a tremendous power that strengthened these Chiotes during times of tribulations. The time of Ottoman rule on the island was the most oppressive. The Turks definitely made violent attempts to change the faith of the Christians. The results were exactly the opposite of what the enemy expected. The people of Chios proceeded to make a bold confession of faith, which led many of their elect sons and daughters to a glorious martyrdom. Their sacrifice rekindled the faith and bonded the people closer to the Church. Today on the island of Chios, there are about one thousand sacred altars of worship, more than one hundred parishes, about eight hundred country chapels, and twenty monastic churches, such as the one providing hospitality to us now. All of these reveal and prove impressively the extent of the Orthodox Christian faith of the people of Chios.

Below we will refer briefly to the martyrs of Chios during the Turkish period of domination. The first of these was Andrew Argentis. He was born in Chios in 1438 to a noble family that was pious and virtuous. He became sick at an early age and almost died. With fervent and heartfelt prayer, he recovered with help from the Panaghia. While Andrew was still young, his father sent him to Constantinople for commercial reasons. He became involved in the commerce of silk fabrics. His competitors in this trade slandered him to the Turkish authorities, saying that he had denied his Islamic identity. Andrew attempted in vain to prove his innocence. He was imprisoned. Invitations, promises, gifts, and honors received from the Turks left Andrew indifferent and unmoved. By no means were they able to change his Orthodox faith. They tied him with chains, beat him, abused him, and tortured him to no avail. The martyrdom continued as his shoulders were seared with a burning iron. In a strange and miraculous manner, with the help again of Panaghia, whom he constantly beseeched, his wounds healed quickly. The executioners became angered and began to cut his flesh with razors and to submit him to other horrific tortures. In the end they beheaded him on May 29, 1465. He was then twenty-seven years old. He was buried in the crypt of the Church of Panaghia Odegetria in Constantinople. Later in Chios, during the Turkish period, churches were built in his honor. One young man of Chios, handsome, educated, wealthy, intelligent, industrious, gave his life fearlessly for Christ. He could have avoided the martyrdom: he could have lied; he could have accepted the honors offered to him. But he did not yield to the temptation. He did not betray his faith, and this meant the loss of his life. For this reason he is a significant, heroic, glorious new martyr.

St. Nicholas the New Martyr was born in Karyes of Chios in 1731 to pious parents. His father died when Nicholas was a young boy, but he grew up with a good Christian education provided by his mother. At the age of twenty he went with a fellow villager to the area of Asia Minor directly across from Chios. He worked with his friend as a builder in Magnesia. As a young man he was distinguished by his seriousness, his reverence, his humility, his simplicity, his goodness, his forbearance, and his meekness. He never responded to provocations, and he was always peaceful and patient. He was a good example of a good, Christian young man. Suddenly something happened to him, and he closed in on himself and did not speak much, and as a result a few unscrupulous individuals exploited him. They even led him to the judge, on the grounds that he had allegedly betrayed the Islamic religion. The judge, receiving no answer from Nicholas, allowed him to go free. Nicholas then returned to his island and his home. For a period of time, he worked as a shepherd in the mountains. With the help of God and the prayers read for him by a priest, Nicholas rediscovered his spiritual health. Some people, however, considered him to be a Muslim, having changed his religion in Anatolia, and they called him Mehmeti. He was indifferent to such remarks and continued to attend church, even though some of the Christians would send him away as a betrayer of the faith. One day when the church was filled with people, he felt compelled to shout, "I am a Christian, and as a Christian I shall die!" The Turks later seized him, imprisoned him, and tortured him severely. During the time of his imprisonment, he fasted and prayed constantly, rejecting every alluring proposal made by the Turks that he deny his Orthodox faith. In the end he was beheaded on October 31, 1754, at the age of twenty-three. After the beheading of the new martyr, darkness fell suddenly upon the island, and his relic alone shone with light. Other miraculous events were also reported to have taken place. To prevent the Christians from honoring Nicholas as a new martyr, the Turks threw his relic into the sea, and it was lost. One marvels at the boldness, the courage, and the undaunted faith of one young man, one of your fellow countrymen, one of your ancestors.

St. Demetrios the New Martyr was born at Palaiokastro of Chios in 1780 to pious parents. He and his brother went to Constantinople to work. There his brother got married, while later he himself also got engaged, but without the opinion and blessing of his brother. This angered the brother, who sent Demetrios away from their home. Going then to a Turkish client who owed him money, he met with the client's daughter, who had fallen in love with Demetrios during previous visitations. She invited him into the house to wait for her father, who was elsewhere and was expected to return. She quickly expressed her desire and passion and told him, "You must become a Turk, or they will cut your head off!" Perplexed and frightened, he agreed and remained in their household for two months. Soon after that, in repentance and with many tears, he began to think of ways to escape his predicament. During the period of Ramadan, he found the opportune time to depart. He went to the home of a Christian friend. He also went to a priest and made his confession. He reconciled with his married brother and wrote his story to their parents. With fasting and prayer he prepared himself for the expected martyrdom, and with much contrition he prayed for the forgiveness of his great sin of temporarily denying Christ. He presented himself before the judge and without hesitation confessed his Christian faith. He remained steadfast in this faith even after imprisonment and torture. People from Chios in the service of the Porte (the central government) collected funds to buy his release from prison. Demetrios was troubled by this and asked that the money be given to the churches and to have prayers said for him. With extraordinary courage and while praying, he was beheaded on

January 29, 1802, at the age of twenty-two. The Christians managed to take his sacred relics and to bury them in the Monastery of the Transfiguration on the island of Proti in Propontis, where many miracles were accomplished through him.

The Hieromartyr Dorotheos Proios was born in Chios, where he received his early education. Later he studied at the School of Patmos and also at various places in Europe. He became friends with Adamantios Korais. He returned to his native Chios as a scholar and then went on to Constantinople. In 1805 he was ordained Metropolitan of Philadelphia. In 1811 he was registered as a monk in the Monastery of Nea Moni in Chios. In 1813 he was elected Metropolitan of Andrianoupolis. He offered good and faithful service wherever he served the Church. Together with other hierarchs he was hanged for his faith at the Mega Rema of Constantinople on June 2, 1821. Dorotheos Proios is a martyr of the Church and a great teacher of the nation. He is considered to be one of many who contributed to the educational rebirth of modern Hellenism just before the War of Independence in 1821. He introduced mathematics in the schools. He loved and promoted study and education among his students and his faithful people.

St. George the New Martyr was born in Pityos of northern Chios in 1785. He was very young when his mother died. He went to be an assistant in the shop of a woodcarver. They went together to the island of Psara to prepare an *iconostasion*. One day George and his friends secretly sailed to Kavala in a fishing boat. While there he took some watermelons from somewhere without permission. He was seized for this and, fearing the consequences before the Turks, denied his faith. He returned to his native island in shame over his serious transgression. After telling his father the story, the father himself escorted the son to the priest of the village. He advised the young man accordingly and directed him to distance himself from the island for the time being. He went with his father to Aivali and there stayed with a Christian family in order to work. There he made progress and was loved by all. At the age of twenty-two, he was engaged to a nice young lady. Her brother, however, reported him to the Turks as one who had denied their faith. Even though dear friends alerted him in time and he could have escaped or hidden, he did not do so. He had no difficulty saying to his judges, "Christianity cannot be undone by the sword, nor by hanging or anything else, because it is the cornerstone of the world!" He was then imprisoned and endured various tortures. Secretly in prison he made his final confession and received Holy Communion for the last time. All the Christians kept an all-night vigil to pray for him. He was beheaded on November 26, 1807. He too was only twenty-two years old. He often appeared in the dreams of his fiancée to console and help her.

The new martyrs mentioned above were born in Chios. The ones mentioned below passed through Chios and will be presented even more briefly. The New Martyr Theophilos was from Zakynthos and worked as a sailor. He came to Chios on a ship. He was accused of denying Islam. For his persistence in his Orthodox Christian faith, he suffered martyrdom on July 24, 1635. He was burned alive at the age of eighteen.

The New Martyr Niketas was born in Nisyros, where he and his entire family changed their religion and became Muslims. When he grew up, he learned of his family's religious journey. He went first to the Holy Mountain and then to Chios. Here at the Monastery of Nea Moni he made his confession, was instructed in the faith, and was chrismated again, thus beginning an exemplary new Christian life. He also went to the Skete of the Holy Fathers to prepare himself for the expected martyrdom that would certainly come, the desire for which had already been kindled in his young heart. He was beheaded on June 21, 1732. He was only sixteen years old.

There are some references about the New Martyr Athanasios from Kio of Bithynia, who was also martyred in Chios on July 24, 1670.

The New Martyr Markos from Smyrni, who was married in Chios and who temporarily denied his Orthodox faith, lived an adventurous life in various places. In the end, however, he repented and died a martyr's death on June 5, 1801, boldly and fearlessly proclaiming Christ to be the only true God.

The New Martyr Alexander from Thessalonike denied Christ at a young age and eventually became a dervish leader. In the end, however, he repented and came to Chios, where he prepared himself for the martyrdom that eventually occurred on May 26, 1794, in Smyrni.

The New Martyr Manuel from the Sfakia of Crete was captured by the Turks and was forcefully converted to Islam. He later managed to escape from his captors and flee to Mykonos, where he married and had six children. When he was informed that his wife was not faithful, he took the children and abandoned her. Her brother, however, informed the Turkish authorities that he had forsaken their faith. He was then brought to Chios and there suffered martyrdom on March 15, 1792.

The New Martyr Theodore the Byzantios was misled and converted to Islam at a young age. He later repented sincerely and came to Chios, where Makarios Notaras and Nikephoros of Chios prepared him for martyrdom. He later ended up in Mytilene, and there, after many severe tortures, he was finally hanged on February 17, 1795, at the age of twenty-one.

The New Martyr Onouphrios from the Great Tirnovo of Bulgaria had also denied the faith from a young age. After repenting later in life, he went to the Holy Mountain and became a monk. There he was well prepared for his glorious martyrdom, which finally took place in Chios on January 1, 1818. He was thirty-two years old.

The New Martyr Polydoros from Leukosia of Cyprus was a merchant who traveled to many different places. Once he became drunk and, without realizing what he was doing, changed his faith and became a Muslim. After recovering and realizing what he had done during his drunkenness, he repented immediately. He confessed with fervent tears, received the sacrament of Chrismation again, and ended up in Chios, where he eventually endured many tortures and died a martyr's death on September 3, 1794.

The New Martyr Angelis was from Argos in the Peloponnesos, and he practiced medicine as a doctor. For some unknown reason he changed his faith. He came to Chios and attended church services there. According to his hagiography in the Menaion, he would wet the holy icons with his tears as he reverenced them and expressed his profound repentance. He fulfilled his repentance by countersigning his Orthodox faith with the blood of his martyrdom on December 3, 1813.

St. Demetrios the New Martyr came from Triphylia of the Peloponnesos. He was forced and pressured to change his faith at a young age in Tripoli. After repenting sincerely, he came to Chios, and there he was prepared for martyrdom by experienced spiritual fathers. Finally he died a martyr's death back in Tripoli on April 14, 1803.

The new martyr brothers Stamatios and John, and their companion Nicholas from the island of Spetsai in the Saronikos, were martyred at the place of the slaughterhouses in Chios on February 3, 1822. Stamatios was twenty-two years old, and John was only eighteen.

A total of eighteen new martyrs were martyred on the island of Chios. Most of them were considerably young in age. I think that this alone has something to say to our young people today. Glory be to God that today we do not have persecutions. What significance does the sacrifice of all these people on your island have, and certainly the sacrifice of so many others in all parts of Greece? Do we listen to these things today with indifference? Does their sacrifice not have something to say to us too? Did they make a mistake in defending and upholding their faith? If something similar were to happen today in our life, what would we do? Would we look to find the best place to hide? Or would we easily deny our faith? Perhaps I am posing difficult questions. On the eve of our National Independence Day, the dual celebration of March 25 as a religious and a patriotic commemoration, it is worthwhile, my beloved young people, to think a little more deeply, a little more seriously. The martyrdom of the new martyrs of Chios did not glorify and sanctify only the martyrs themselves; their martyrdom became a source of inspiration, renewed strength, and encouragement for many of their fellow patriots of the same Orthodox faith. First of all and primarily, many became more determined not to ever deny or change their faith, but to repent sincerely and to regain their faith, if they had in some way or under adverse circumstances denied or lost it.

The wise commentators say that nations without memory die out. The legs of a nation are its language and its religious faith. If these legs are cut off, a nation will not be able to move forward and will be lost. Today, unfortunately, we are sometimes embarrassed to admit that we are Orthodox Christians, to make the sign of the cross, to confess our faith. The Church must be looked at again more carefully and more seriously so that all of her depth and fullness might be seen and appreciated. The Church is not a philanthropic society or a social organization, but a tender maternal embrace. We never reject anyone, whatever he may believe; we support that which the past generations have transmitted to us with their blood. Contemporary intellectuals, however, are proclaiming stridently that atheism is now fashionable. Orthodoxy is the most progressive faith. It is a faith for demanding persons, for those who are particularly intelligent and bold, and who are seeking perfection and fullness in their life. We must see again the message of the Church clearly, without colored glasses. Perhaps we too are to blame, because, with our particular ways, we did not help you to be inspired by the most-beautiful truth of the gospel.

The great Russian author Dostoyevsky used to say, "I will not replace Christ with anything!" General Makriyiannis, who had five serious wounds on his body from the War of Independence, would say with pain, "The religion and the fatherland of every person is the most important thing; nations cannot stand without virtue and suffering for the fatherland, and without faith and love for the religion." The first Governor of Greece, John Kapodistrias, used to say, "The primary and most essential duty of the Greek government is to provide the nation with the teaching of the faith."

Today, unfortunately, my young people, many are they who seem to be mocking the Orthodox Faith; they consider it to be too austere, old-fashioned, confined to external forms, and not something for young people. Speaking about Orthodoxy, we do not mean at all—and this is the truth—religious superstitions, fanaticism, extremism, oppressiveness, constant prohibitions, large crosses, and stupid pseudo-piety. Orthodoxy gives meaning to life; it gives specific and critical goals, correctness in our way of life, fearlessness before the reality of death, and the melting away of frozen loneliness, which usually comes from a cruel and unyielding egotism. The lack of a healthy humility creates in our young men and women many psychological, spiritual, and even physical problems. Orthodoxy beautifies and gives meaning to the life of those who have high hopes and aspirations and a profound sense of their existence as human beings.

Love for the country, for which both the heroes of 1821 and the new martyrs sacrificed themselves, is not at all a matter of a sickly nationalism, racism, or rejecting foreigners. Knowledge of country and love for country are certainly beautiful qualities in themselves. Without fear of foreigners, without confinement within our own selves, without isolation and mistrust, we are called to study well our history, which has produced a marvelous civilization of three thousand five hundred years with a truly rich contribution to the world.

It is truly of great worth and value to look again at things more deeply, more seriously, more responsibly. A timely orientation upon sublime and sound foundations is indispensable. Elder Paisios of the Holy Mountain used to say, "I have so much joy that I do not know what to do with it!" He was speaking a truth. He was not simply trying to enthuse. He was saying what he was actually and truly experiencing. We are all created for joy. True joy is not in staying up all night, in drinking and dancing at parties, in drugs, in carnal pleasures and material possessions. True joy is in the spirit. The youth of a nation are created for a heroic life. The new martyrs of your island are also certainly motivating you to this heroic life, in which I wish and pray that you will always be truly joyful.

5

THE ALL-HOLY THEOTOKOS

IN THE ORTHODOX CHURCH THE PLACE OF OUR ALL-HOLY LADY, the Theotokos and ever-virgin Mary, is especially sublime. According to St. John of Damascus, she holds the second place after the Holy Trinity. We Orthodox Christians, after the honor we give to the Holy Trinity, honor the all-virtuous and all-holy Theotokos.

The divine and holy evangelists refer to her in the Gospels with exceeding reverence and love, especially St. Luke. The person of the Theotokos is presented in the Gospels as a model and example of a faithful woman, called to salvation in the faith and grace of God. She holds an exceptional position within the Church. She is the beautiful, modest, humble maiden who totally accepted the divine Word with complete faith. In contrast to the first Eve, Mary is obedient to the divine will, to the divine calling, in its most perfect form.

The Theotokos is indeed the unique Mother of God and of mankind. She is indeed a singularly sacred person and unrepeatable. She represents the very best that humanity had to offer to God. In her person divinity found modesty, humility, purity, chastity, and obedience, in their most appropriate and extraordinary form. The all-holy Theotokos stands in that particular personal condition that does not belong to any other member of the

Church. She is the only virgin mother. She is the Mother of the Lord through her free will. She freely accepted bearing the Son and Logos of God for the people of God, the people whom she actually represents and whom she unites to this acceptance of salvation offered by God. Thus Christ is the new Adam, and the all-holy Theotokos is the new Eve.

The Fathers of the Church indicate the footsteps of the Theotokos in all of the Old Testament. They speak beautifully about prefiguration and preformulation. The first proclamation about her honorable person comes with the so-called "protoevangelion"—the first announcement of good news. When God declares to the serpent-demon that He will set enmity between him and the woman, He is referring to the Panaghia, the all-holy Theotokos. She will be the one to bear the fruit that will eventually crush the head of the dragon that merely wounds the heel of her son.

Another image is that of the burning bush. This is the bush that the Prophet Moses the God-seer saw on the God-trodden Mount Sinai. The bush was burning but was not consumed. For the great dogmatic theologian of our Church, St. John of Damascus, the unconsumed burning bush is a prefiguration of the Theotokos and of the presence of the divine light coming to us through the virgin maiden. St. Gregory Palamas, who writes with great love about the Theotokos, speaks of the uncreated light, the glory of the Lord, which is the manifestation of Christ in the world. The light came out of the Theotokos, who was not harmed by the birth of the Savior.

One more superb image is the ladder that the Patriarch Jacob saw in his dream. He saw a ladder connecting the earth with heaven. According to the patristic interpretation, this ladder is the Theotokos. God descended this ladder to come to earth. The Theotokos became the bridge to unite what had been separated. We express this beautifully in the Akathistos Hymn: "Rejoice, O Bridge, transferring those on earth to heaven; Rejoice, O heavenly Ladder, by which God has descended."

The great prophet Isaiah uses the term "the staff of Jesse" to refer to the Theotokos. What does he mean? He calls the Virgin

Mary a branch from the staff of Jesse (Isa 11:1). Jesse was the father of Judah, from whose tribe and generation the Virgin Mary was born. He therefore calls her a branch from the spiritual tree that was raised up by Jesse, and from which came the flower: Christ. Another very well-known prophecy of Isaiah is the one we read at the Nativity of Christ: "Behold, the virgin shall conceive and bear a Son, and you shall call His name Immanuel" (7:14). This same important prophet gave us also the prophecy we hear at Pascha: "Shine, shine, O Jerusalem, for your light has come, and the glory of the Lord has dawned upon you" (60:1).

The annual ecclesial cycle of celebrations for the person of the Mother of God begins in the month of September and ends in August. On September 8 we commemorate the Birth of the All-Holy Theotokos. This festal event is not recorded in the New Testament; it comes from the deuterocanonical Gospel that is attributed to the Apostle James. The parents of Mary are the virtuous and God-fearing Joachim and Anna. The infertility of St. Anna saddened her as well as her good and virtuous husband Joachim. In the Old Testament infertility was considered to be an expression of God's disfavor and therefore endured in shame. We observe the elderly couple praying fervently for God to grand them a child. This is indicative of their profound faith in divine assistance. After all, they have many examples from history motivating them in their request: Sarah, the mother of Isaac; Anna, the mother of Samuel; Elizabeth, the mother of John. But why was infertility considered to be so shameful? Because the woman who did not bear children did not serve and contribute to the coming of the Savior (D. Mavropoulos).

The Panaghia Mary was born through the union of a man and a woman and not by an "immaculate conception," as some Westerners say. She was born as all of us are born. St. John of Damascene refers to the parents of the Theotokos as "blessed spouses." Our Church is most grateful to them for their unique contribution. They are commemorated in the dismissal prayer of every sacrament and service. The Panaghia was born with good qualities and virtuous advantages and considerable heavenly powers and graces, all of which she preserved, cultivated, and increased. With her willing self-consciousness she accepted the divine calling and consented wholeheartedly to the divine will. She cooperates consciously and is associated with both heaven and earth.

The feast of the Entrance into the Temple of the Theotokos, on November 21, is of great significance. First of all, it is a most moving and remarkable and amazing fact that the elderly parents did not keep the gift of God, the elect daughter acquired at the setting of their life, egotistically close, to serve and to care for them in their old age. Rather, having a presentiment of her future sublime and salutary service to the Benevolent God's plan for the redemption of the entire human race, they offer her without reservations to the temple of God, to the holy of holies. The young daughter does not oppose, does not react with another will; she has no fear and is not tied to her parents, even though she loves them very much. Her parents too are not tied to their daughter in a sickly manner, though they love her dearly, because they see clearly that she is destined for another place. We marvel and are inspired by the obedience of the innocent little girl, who remains alone, at such a tender age, in the temple for thirteen years. She enters the temple at three and receives the Annunciation at the age of sixteen.

Her stay in the temple for thirteen years is a truly marvelous event. The holy maiden remains vigilant in the holy of holies of the sacred temple, praying, fasting, studying, preparing herself, and experiencing the virtues. She loves holiness, cleanliness, modesty, humility, simplicity, frugality, and contentment in few things, particularly prayer and silence. She does not play, does not speak idly, is not negligent, and does not lose time with secondary and unnecessary things. She does not seek to find something. She lives, experiences, and enjoys, and her soul abides in gladness. She does not complain, is not stressed, has no fear, and is not in a hurry. She has abandoned herself to the divine will and has identified her will with the divine will. She lives in paradise, freely, as did Eve before the fall. She has no worries, no misfortunes, no superficialities, no reservations, and no ulterior motives. She has completely, honorably, and joyfully given herself to God. This is why Mary, the all-virtuous Panaghia, is significant, exceptional, amazing, and extraordinarily unique.

When each night we say, during the most-beautiful prayer service of Compline, the laudatory adjectives to the Theotokos: "spotless, immaculate, chaste, undefiled, pure, virgin, bride of God," we do not say them with a literary and poetic disposition. These adjectives are not meant, as among Western Christians, as given gifts, but rather as conscientious activities of the Panaghia herself. The Panaghia could sin, but she did not want to sin. She had the ancestral sin, the sinful tendency to easily slip, but with her pure and sound faith and her complete trust in God, she did not ever will to sin. With all her being she hated evil, sin, passions, malice, and irreverence. She loved the good, the virtuous, the sacred; everything that is beautiful, moral, God-pleasing, loved by God, and superlatively virtuous.

After the feast day of the Entrance, we have next in order the feast of the Annunciation. The event is well known, and we will not extend our analysis and become redundant. We will focus only on a few significant points. The Archangel Gabriel, sent from heaven, appears to the Virgin Mary and informs her that she will give birth to the Savior of the world. The announcement alone is incredibly shocking, frightful, and heard for the first time. The response of the humble maiden, according to the Evangelist Luke, was "Behold the maidservant of the Lord! Let it be to me according to your word" (Luke 1:38). The knowledgeable interpreters of Scripture make a noteworthy distinction. In Hebrew the word for "servant" does not have the usual meaning of serving another, but of working with someone as a co-worker. Thus the response of the Virgin Mary meant her free consent to cooperate in the great mystery of the divine Incarnation. The all-holy Virgin was not one without a will, small-minded, naïve, careless, or unsuspecting. When Mary asked, "How can this be, since I do not know a man?" she knew what she was talking about; she was thinking seriously and clearly, and spoke attentively, without losing her composure. When the archangel reassured her that this would happen through the coming of the Holy Spirit, she then became peaceful and serene; she consented and accepted the divine will. God does not force, prevail over, overwhelm, and violate human free will. God respects it absolutely, since He Himself has granted this exceptional gift of free will to man. The acceptance of the divine will by man is indicative of his cooperation and participation. The service offered by the all-holy Virgin Mary is indeed sublime and of the highest quality, for she is offering and placing herself in the service of God for the salvation of the world. She thus becomes a co-worker in the saving work of God for the world.

The dismissal hymn for the feast says, "Today is the beginning of our salvation, and the manifestation of the mystery of old; the Son of God is becoming the Son of man." The Panaghia is the beginning of our salvation. It is very difficult to comprehend and to understand fully the great magnitude of the Theotokos' most sublime contribution to the world. The more one becomes cleansed and purified, the more he will understand something more and experience the compunction of many grateful tears. The Fathers of the Church who practiced hesychasm had a special love for the feast of the Annunciation, as did the neo-hesychasts and holy Fathers known as the Kollyvades, who lived on this island with great love for the saints. Your blessed bishop and most pious elder Hierotheos has written beautifully about these saintly Kollyvades Fathers, who built churches wherever they went and dedicated them to the Annunciation of the Theotokos.

An interesting and moving image from the God-filled life of the Theotokos is her meeting with St. Elizabeth, the mother of the Forerunner. In her greeting to Elizabeth, the Panaghia declared her voluntary cooperation in the salvation of the human race and her profound understanding of the events occurring in the mystery of the divine economy. According to the Evangelist Luke, at the moment when Elizabeth heard the greeting of Mary, she felt the baby in her womb, St. John the Forerunner, leap with joy. Filled with the Holy Spirit, Elizabeth spoke to the Panaghia and said aloud, "Blessed are you among women, and blessed is the fruit of your womb. But why is this granted to me, that the mother of my Lord should come to me? For indeed, as soon as the voice of your greeting sounded in my ears, the babe leaped in my womb for joy. Blessed is she who believed, for there will be a fulfillment of those things which were told her from the Lord" (Luke 1:42–45).

At that moment, the Virgin Mary took the opportunity and spoke joyfully the following hymn of praise:

> My soul magnifies the Lord,
>   and my spirit rejoices in God my Savior,
>   for he has regarded the lowly state of His maidservant.
> For behold, henceforth all generations will call me blessed;
> For almighty God has done great things for me,
>   and holy is His name;
> And His mercy is on those who fear Him
>   from generation to generation.
> He has shown strength with His arm;
> He has scattered the proud in the imagination of their hearts.
> He has put down the mighty from their thrones,
>   and exalted the lowly.
> He has filled the hungry with good things,
>   and the rich He has sent away empty.
> He has helped His servant Israel,
>   in remembrance of His mercy,
>   as He spoke to our fathers,
>   to Abraham and to his descendants forever. (Luke 1:46–55)

Mary stayed and visited with Elizabeth for three months.

Exactly nine months after the Annunciation, Mary gave birth in Bethlehem to the divine Child. Divine providence provided for the supernatural birth of the Lord the appropriate conditions to protect both the life and reputation of the Virgin Mary and of the newborn Child. It is within this secure and protective plan that the betrothal of the Virgin Mary to the righteous and virtuous Joseph is to be placed, and this betrothal truly offered many significant things. It protected the Virgin Mary from moral denigration and prevented slanderous comments at her expense. The law was very strict regarding an "unfaithful" betrothed, and spoke of divorce or even of death by stoning. The angel of the Lord had informed Joseph that the Virgin's conception was the fruit of the Holy Spirit. Thus Joseph the Betrothed stood firmly as the guardian and protector of his betrothed and an important servant in the mystery of the Incarnation of the Savior. For this reason, the blessed elder of Patmos, Amphilochios Makris, felt a particular reverence for St. Joseph and had a church built in his name, to honor his great service to the Theotokos.

St. John Chrysostom emphasizes in one of his homilies an important point about the mystery of the Incarnation. The mystery is known only through faith and cannot be researched through rationalistic scrutiny. The mystery is revered by bowing in awe before it; we do not attempt to measure it by rational standards, nor to submit it to natural reasoning. The mystery is confessed, not measured. It is not a natural mystery but a supernatural one. In another place, St. John Chrysostom continues in the same vein, God became man to deify us; He became poor to make us rich. To be born, God did not seek out a palace, nor a rich mother from some prominent lineage; He chose rather a poor young maiden, betrothed to a righteous carpenter. The Evangelist Luke refers to the Panaghia as a virgin betrothed to Joseph (1:27). Elsewhere the same evangelist refers to her as the wife of Joseph (2:5). According to the social customs of that time in Judaism, a betrothed woman was considered to be the wife of the man she was betrothed to. The betrothal was an essential and binding institution, and not merely a formal relationship. If the betrothed man died, his betrothed became his widow. Also, the breaking of a betrothal could only be done by means of a divorce (M. G. Angelides).

The Prophet Isaiah, eight centuries before Christ, said, "The Virgin shall conceive and bear a Son, and you shall call His name Immanuel" (Isa 7:14). This event is properly called a beginning and an end: the beginning of salvation and the end of perdition. Eusebius of Caesarea, commenting on the prophetic passage of Isaiah, says, "This message was never heard before throughout all the ages—a Virgin bearing a Son, who is God and Savior of the human race! The rationalists, of course, mock such incredible things, including the miracle of the ever-virginity of the Theotokos." To this St. John Chrysostom responds marvelously, "Do not seek to know the *how*. Where God wills, the order of nature is overcome. This is the way God chose to will and to act; He descended and saved. All things always support and assist God." Elsewhere St. John continues, "Christ was born of the Virgin. The manner of the birth I have learned to honor by silence and not with overly verbose curiosity. The nature of the supernatural event causes me to keep a dignified silence."

St. Basil the Great refers to the Virgin Mary as being truly ever-virgin. The Prophet Zacharias also placed the Panaghia, after the birth of the Lord, with the virgins. This is why the Jews killed him between the temple and the altar of sacrifice. It was impossible for them to understand how a mother could also be a virgin. Christ was born without seed, and the virginity of the Theotokos remained inviolate. It is a miracle of the greatest magnitude—unique, unheard of, and unrepeatable. It is like the sun that passes with its rays through the glass of the window without harming it.

My beloved, it is worthwhile to pause for a moment at the first miracle of the Lord at the wedding of Cana, where both His mother and His disciples were present. The beautiful narrative is recorded in the Gospel of St. John. At some point during the wedding feast, the wine for the guests ran out. Jesus' mother was the first to make this observation. She approached Jesus and told Him that there was no more wine. He appeared to be sharp with her, as if she were interfering prematurely with His work. She, of course, was not at all troubled, and merely advised the servants to do whatever He told them to do. Jesus instructed the servants to fill the six large vessels standing there with water to the brim, and then to take some to the master of the feast. When the master of the feast tasted the water that had now become very good wine, he was delighted and exclaimed that he had never before had such good wine. The evangelist informs us that this was the beginning of the signs/miracles that Jesus started to do. Please note that the first miracle of Christ was not the healing of some sick person—a paralytic, or a blind or possessed person—but rather the offering of simple domestic joy. He turned the water into wine so that the joy of the invited guests at the wedding would be complete. In this regard the intervention of the Theotokos is most significant. She urges, pleads, beseeches, and prays constantly for those who are in need. She is the joy of all, the hope of the hopeless, and the helper of all. She bows to the ear of Christ and asks Him to help us. We could perhaps say, if permissible, that we Orthodox are very fortunate to have this ease in calling upon the Lady Theotokos. The earlier fathers of the Holy Mountain used to say with certainty and knowledge, "Whatever the Panaghia asks from Christ, He will do it, because He loves her very much."

The presence of the Theotokos at the wedding of Cana is therefore particularly significant. We could even say that the intervention of the Theotokos, her appeal to her Son to change the water into wine, symbolizes the successful conclusion of various familial circumstances and problems and is thus a secure and given precedent. In a sense, then, the Theotokos promises to the newly wedded couple—to those who submit their life to Christ, her Son—that she will always intercede so that Christ will fulfill their requests and offer them whatever is necessary for their family and their salvation.

At the scene of the Crucifixion of the Lord on the horrible Golgotha, the presence of the Theotokos is not merely emotional but actually shocking and most instructive. The beloved disciple of the Lord, St. John the Theologian, who saw and heard what happened there, describes the scene as a firsthand witness. Under the Cross there were three women with the same name, Mary: the mother of Jesus and ever-virgin Mary, Mary the wife of Cleopas, and Mary Magdalene. The frightened disciples were hiding. Only John was there. He was standing next to the Panaghia, providing the comfort she needed at her Son's martyrdom, which had brought deep sorrow to her heart. One of the hymns says that a sword cut through her all-holy soul. At this final hour and in His own agonizing pain, Christ is thinking of His mother and her own maternal pain. And as He speaks to her and nods toward the beloved disciple, He says, "There, he will from now on be your son." And to avoid any doubt or uncertainty, He speaks to the disciple and says, "From now on she will be your mother." From that hour John took Panaghia with him to his house and cared for her. He loved Christ, and he loved His mother. It is not possible to believe and to love Christ and not to also honor and respect His mother, the Panaghia. One cannot love the Panaghia without loving Christ. The Panaghia always leads us and unites us with Christ.

John has recorded Jesus' words to His mother and to himself, but not for historical reasons or as a tribute of honor to himself. They have a dimension, an extension, a lesson, that is serious and significant. It is a powerful experience that is realized within the realm of the life of the Church. John says that he took the Theotokos to his own (τὰ ἴδια). This does not mean simply his home, but rather a particular space that is his own, a clean, well-prepared, and adorned place. What place is that? This is our heart, a truly loved and familiar place. By telling His mother to become mother to John, it is as if Christ is speaking also to us. We are to make His mother our mother. John in turn is urging us to become His brothers and to all have the same loving mother, the mother of the Savior. In order to become her children, we are called to take her into our "home," to appropriate her as our own mother, to love her and her godly virtues, and to imitate her life so that in us too, within us, there may be born the Christ, who is the life, the light, and the salvation of the world.

The blessed elder Theokletos Dionysiates has said that for one to write and talk about the Theotokos, "one must be an enlightened, holy, high-minded, and broad-minded theologian, and, if not, he should not write anything of his own, but simply transcribe by selecting what the holy theologians have written." This is how it is and this is how we are attempting to write about the Theotokos. In his laudatory homily on the Dormition of the Theotokos, the final feast day for the Mother of God, St. Gregory

Palamas declares that the death of the Theotokos is a life-bearing death that leads to an immortal life. The celebration of this sorrowful event thus becomes a bright festival. It reminds us of the miracles of the Theotokos, her virtuous adornment, and the presence of angels, apostles, and other saints at her glorious Dormition. The presence of God Himself renders to His mother, who is most chaste and wholly without evil, the most appropriate honor at her departure from this life. The God-bearing St. Gregory says beautifully that the Theotokos made God into the Son of man, and men into sons of God. Thus she made earth into heaven, deified humanity, and honored the nature of women. The Theotokos marked out the citizens of earth and destined them to become heavenly beings. She became the spiritual queen of the human race. In the end, the earth, the tomb, and death itself could not hold down her God-bearing and God-holding body. Thus our Theotokos was transferred, in body and soul, from earth to heaven, in spite of the various reasoned and rationalistic opinions of certain modern theologians.

Thus the feast day is filled with joy and gladness. The transfer of the Theotokos to heaven brings gladness to those who before were mourning over death. The incomparable and God-motivated hymnology of the Church emphasizes for us the Dormition and transfer of the all-holy Theotokos. An angel of the Lord God foretold her exodus from this world. The Panaghia, rejoicing over this foretelling, went to the Mount of Olives to pray. She returned to her home, waiting for her departure and the appearance of her Son. Then a great, thunderous sound occurred, and in a miraculous manner the apostles gathered from the ends of the inhabited world and appeared in Gethsemane to bury the body of the all-immaculate one. She reclined upon her bed in the usual manner and delivered her soul into the hands of her Son. The apostles buried her body, but on the third day it was no longer found in the tomb. The Apostle Thomas, with his good disbelief and curiosity, opened the tomb to reverence the holy relic of the all-immaculate mother and found nothing but the burial sheets. God had transferred her to heaven. This account is written about the Dormition and Metastasis (Translation) of the Theotokos in the important Menologion document of Basil II dating from the tenth century.

This significant description serves as the basis for the iconographic representation of the Dormition with its many persons, among whom the Theotokos, asleep on her bed, dominates the scene; meanwhile, the Lord, high above, holds her soul—an all-pure white dove—depicted as a pure and innocent little infant girl. Surrounding the bier are apostles and holy hierarchs, while archangels and angels descend from heaven. It is true that the feast of the Dormition of the Theotokos dominates all the feasts of the Theotokos and is in fact called "the Summer Pascha." The faithful go to the shrines, fill the churches, and keep vigils; they pray, beseech, supplicate, appeal to, and thank the Mother of God. Innumerable are the offerings at the miraculous icons of the Theotokos with a myriad of characteristically beautiful names.

St. John of Damascus says that as long as there are people, they will bless the Theotokos, for she is the one who is, before all others, worthy of every blessing and praise. The angels transferred her into heaven, and even the air was sanctified. The angelic powers in heaven receive into the heavenly domains with superb hymns; she is the one who is "more honorable than the Cherubim, and more glorious beyond compare than the Seraphim." In his eloquent praise of the Theotokos, the saint asks poetically, "How can heaven receive the one who has become broader than the heavens? And how has the tomb received the one who received God in her womb? O sacred tomb, marvelous and respected and revered, adorned by angels who even now are present with much respect and awe, while faithful human beings come to praise, to reverence, and to kiss it and with eyes and lips, thus drawing, with deep emotion of soul, abundant blessings."

The excellent lover of the Theotokos, St. John of Damascus, continues his eloquent references to the unique queen of the heavens and of earth: "You have become a blessing for the entire world, a sanctification for the universe, rest for the weary, consolation for the mourners, healing for the sick, a haven for the storm-tossed in the sea of life, forgiveness for the sinners, encouragement for the suffering, one ready to help all those who call upon you, the beginning, the middle, and the end of all those good things that surpass our mind."

Protestant Christians are, unfortunately, deprived of all these gifts—of the protection, the consolation, and assistance of the Theotokos—by not calling upon her, by not honoring her, and by instead ignoring her. We Orthodox Christians love her and honor her, of course, but the best honor we can offer to her, according to St. John Chrysostom, is for the one who praises her to acquire her mentality and her way of life. It is good to make offerings, to go on pilgrimages and to dedicate ourselves, but it is even better to see things more profoundly. For by remaining on the superficial external surface of things, the mere gifts and visitations, we by necessity remain on the level of easy and painless works. We do not dig deeply within our soul; we do not cultivate diligently our inner garden, with contemplation, with contrition, with self-knowledge, with self-examination, with self-correction, and with self-reproach. We remain on the level of a mere furtive passage, a leisurely stroll, a constant observance of others with an austere glance, while avoiding the discreet austerity that is so useful and helpful when applied to ourselves.

This humble bowing and probing within ourselves is a matter of great significance and value. The permanent transference of responsibilities to others, the pleasant justification of our beloved self, the usual comparison with those who are worse off, the superficial delaying to take action—all these things will certainly and seriously hinder us from progressing in our spiritual ascent and will leave us either spiraling downward or in the boredom of standing still, simply marking time. The wonderful stance of the Theotokos should always censure our inactivity. With kindness, love, and abundant discretion, she presents to us her beautiful, chaste, luminous, and graceful person for the purpose of imitation. In a society of unbridled and uninterrupted seeking after pleasure; of frightening arrogance; and of material pursuits for more money, more possessions, more power, more glory, and more selfishness, the modesty, silence, purity, and humility of our all-virtuous and all-holy Theotokos appears to us in very sharp contrast.

The Panaghia was everywhere and always, before all else, a humble person. She was humble not in words or figures, which hide the hypocrisy abhorred by God, but she was truly, authentically, purely, and essentially humble. It was humility, the queen of the virtues, which so adorned Mary and attracted the grace of God that made her become the Mother of the Lord. Her humility was without interruption, permanent, in full vigor, and strong. She loved it and embraced it; she could not and would not live without it. It was a manner of life that was natural, simple, and not made up pretentiously. It was a life without demands, tensions, hurry, disturbances, noise, struggles, anxieties, and tribulations. She carried within her a cloudless heaven filled with the rays of the sun. Her life was a sea without waves, a serene lake, a silent river, a fragrant meadow filled with flowers, a pleasant aromatic garden. She was never anxious to be noticed, honored, given the first place or the first chance to speak; nor to be praised, flattered, or lauded. Thus she did not have any inferiority, fear, insecurity, sleeplessness, worry, giddiness, oddity, peculiarity, misery, nor foolish overpoliteness or foolish, overly pious religiosity. The humility of the Theotokos was her most precious and most luminous adornment, and it reflected the light and the grace of the humble Jesus.

The humility of the Theotokos made her strong enough to endure, to anticipate, to expect, and to follow the shadow of her Son, strong enough to be silent, to pray, to endure, and to always hope. She had no expectation that the apostles would come and consult her, that they would place her first so that she might influence the affairs of the Church to intervene and to do her will. What an excellent human being—how unique, how rare, how superb!

We look upon, bow down before, reverence, and kiss the holy icon of the Virgin Mary and are inspired. The humble maiden of Nazareth has so much to teach to the people of today, who are overweening, arrogant, egotistical, proud, individualistic, selfish, pleasure seeking, inhospitable, unbrotherly, and unphilanthropic, and who prefer to argue and not to bear children. My brothers and sisters, the main problem of contemporary man is not so much the economic crisis but the increased and pervasive projection of pride. Life has become gray, without smiles; it is harsh, cunning, difficult, and unhumbled. The Benevolent God provides many opportunities for us to be tested, tried, and even tempted so that we might become prudent, corrected, changed, redirected, transfigured, exalted, and resurrected, but unfortunately such opportunities pass by unexploited. Sometimes, in fact, a person's difficulties will make him even more harsh and unyielding, thus leaving no disposition at all to be humbled and to repent.

Christ, however, gives grace to those who are humble; He loves the humble even more and blesses them and will place all of them in paradise. Panaghia prays and intercedes for all people, but especially for the humble. Let us ask her fervently now during her feast day to grant us something of her beautiful humility. When we do, then, even if we find ourselves in an economic crisis, or in illness, or in any other difficulty or unemployment, we will have patience, hope, consolation, and optimism. The humility of the Theotokos also has much to teach the women of today. Let us all call upon her, for we all suffer from a lack of humility. Holy humility will provide us with ease, freedom, joy, grace, sanctity, redemption, and a foretaste of the delight in paradise, which will render us without problems, graceful, and truly joyful even in this life.

Unhumbled and proud, contemporary man imagines that he will be happy with the many possessions and the money he amasses, with his carnal enjoyments and the breathless hunt for pleasures, with the endless changing of clothing, of dwelling, of vehicle, and even of spouse. Man wants to be happy and he is not joyful; he is thirsty and he cannot quench his existential thirst; he yearns for peace and quiet, and he is terribly worried, imagining that the material possessions and pleasures will fill his aching and empty heart. This is how our youth are growing up, seeking to find what will provide more money for them, what will provide ephemeral relationships and passing little joys that are really pseudo-joys. This way of life and state of mind becomes clouded; bad habits are developed from a young age; the truth is distorted; irreverence and apostasy are justified; one seeks out the quick and easy way without effort and labor. From an early age the eyes are dimmed and not bright and clear. A terrible hypocrisy, a miserable cunning, an irreverent impiety, the usual endless lies, the deceptive deceptions, the bitter desire to outwit the others, the hurried improvisations, the daily superficiality, the gross mediocrity, the cheap shallowness—all these and more come to reign in our life. Thus daily life becomes a boring, unbearable, and painful routine. The flesh is worshipped, and its worshippers are far too many; the unnatural is considered to be natural, the irrational rational; deception is seen as intelligence; adultery is accepted as a daring accomplishment; and evil cunning is now an art, while honesty and honor are folly and foolishness.

Unfortunately, my beloved brothers and sisters, our time has become very unclean. Thus the immaculate, the more-than-all-chaste, the ever-virgin Theotokos, in such an uncomely cosmos, appears as a stranger, as distanced, as unknown, as far away from us, and—if I may use the term, and please forgive me—as being old-fashioned. Our Panaghia, who is full of grace, who is the ever-virgin bride, did not know a man, did not sin, did not even think of evil, but rather hated whatever is unholy, unchaste, unclean, foul, and mired in evil. Her purity is of a most excellent and most sublime degree, of great authority and validity, and of inaccessible perfection. Her reluctance toward anything unclean and evil was a free choice, a willed decision that she made of her own volition. This breathtaking and wondrous beauty of her virginity has much to say to our world that is gripped by secularism and the pleasures of the flesh.

It is true, however, that in these spiritually lean times of ours—and we must emphasize this—the good friends, the faithful disciples, the prudent followers, and the beloved imitators of the Virgin Mary are not entirely absent. These are the young men and young women with joyful, peaceful, and luminous faces and personalities, those with purity, chastity, and great blessings; these are the monks and nuns with lifelong abstinence; and these are the people in the world who are without guile—the good, virtuous, and disciplined strugglers in the faith who are worthy of our awe. Let us beseech the Lady of the Angels to cleanse the eyes of our souls and bodies, so that we may see our fellow human beings without guile, look up toward heaven as true human beings, and look within ourselves with clarity, humility, and purity.

We are not attempting here to be like the censuring moralists and the ethicists who judge harshly and without compassion. But if we say that our society today is immodest, we would not be, I think, exaggerating. We are recording the reality and are doing this with the hope that our most virtuous Panaghia will assist us to love the virtue that is woven by God, and to hate all forms of evil that are promoted by the devil. The Panaghia's modesty kept her unfailingly humble, permanently pure, seriously silent, noble, compassionate, and also allowed her to bear such beautiful names: she is "Merciful," "Consolation," "Quick to Hear," "Sweet-Kissing," and ever "Guiding," "Hearing," "Saving."

I do not wish to tire you with much more. This much, for those who want to hear and to listen, is enough. The all-virtuous Panaghia is always ready to inspire us toward virtue, to take us by the hand and lead us to Christ, to strengthen us in our struggles for the acquisition of virtue and sanctity; she is ready to wipe away our tears, to alleviate our pains, to intercede with her Son not to censure our actions too severely before the angels, to assist us quickly, to embrace us in her bosom as she did with Christ.

The Panaghia, "holding in her bosom God the Logos Incarnate," presents us to Christ, unites us with Christ. By loving and honoring the Virgin Mary, we love and honor Christ Himself. The stance we take; the degree of respect we have; the gratitude, the thanksgiving, and the love we have for Mary the Mother of God will determine and define the degree of our Orthodox spirituality. It is true that the more we feel powerless, unable, small, and poor in our efforts to praise her many virtues and blessings, the closer we actually come to the truth.

Therefore, we must thank the all-praised Theotokos most fervently, with all of our heart and soul, for not abandoning the world in her most glorious Dormition. She has never abandoned us, in spite of our many indiscretions and unbecoming actions. On the contrary, like a loving, compassionate, and sympathetic mother, she overlooks so much. And through her Dormition and Metastasis, she stands by the heavenly throne of the Savior as a fervent and ceaseless intercessor for all of us—the young, the old, the poor, the wealthy, the sick, the powerless, the ones with little faith, the ones who have gone astray, the ones who have been outwitted and frightened by the devil. The Panaghia does not discriminate, does not uphold and perpetuate rivalries, does not remember that we often forget her and hold it against us. Her embrace is very broad and has room for all of us. Her virtue is so great, abundant, rich, and precious that it is constantly motivating us to imitate her to some degree. Virtue illumines the world, brightens the darkness, and offers sweetness and redemption. The all-virtuous Panaghia is our only hope after God. We thank her most fervently, and we are grateful to her with all of our heart.

Your Eminence, thank you again for the kind invitation; and you, my brothers and sisters, I thank you for being here and for your attention.

6

THE MOST-COMPASSIONATE FATHER

THE LORD'S FAMILIAR PARABLE ABOUT THE PRODIGAL SON (Luke 15:11–32) is considered to be, according to the divine interpreters, like a precious gem or a glowing pearl among the other instructive parables. It is even referred to as the gospel within the Gospel. It has also been well said that if this parable alone were preserved from the entire Gospel, it would suffice to move and guide man to that all-important and saving repentance. The dominant theme in the parable is clearly the great love of the father.

The younger son in the parable plainly and without long introductory explanations demanded his rightful share of the paternal estate. The father—without objections, delays, postponements, justifications, or excuses—divided his property and gave away the portion that belonged to the younger son. What father today, in this time of total freedom, would have done such a thing so simply, directly, and easily? Why did the father act in this way? Did he not love his son? Was he so wearied over him? Did he want to see him go and be at peace? Did he want to avoid constant bickering and arguments? Was this action of the father justified and its psychological impact carefully thought through? Should he not have tried to exhort the son to reconsider, to be more prudent, and to change his mind? Was the father right in giving his son what he asked for? Should he not have sat him down, talked to him, and urged him to rethink his plans, and thus convinced him that he is not yet mature enough to leave the paternal home? Why did he not at least delay his son's departure? He certainly had many reasons to do so. Why does the story of this parable in the Gospel lesson not refer to any of these legitimate concerns and proper questions?

My brothers and sisters, the good and virtuous father could, of course, have raised all of these questions and even many more. He knew very well the character, the psychological condition, the priorities, and the imperfections of his son. He gave him life, nurtured him, and raised him. He knew perfectly his son's nature, his habits, as well as his strong and weak characteristics. He apparently did not act as all of us would have acted. In fact, we observe another stance, an entirely different attitude of the father, one that is subversive and terribly upsetting to us. Here now we will surely have severe objections. Are we not, then, to teach our children, to try to convince them of what is best for them to do? Should we not teach them to avoid evil and to do good? Should we not instruct them to be obedient and submissive to what we teach them?

My dear brothers, I did not write the parable. Christ Himself gave us this parable, and it is impeccable and whole as it is. If it needed more words, the author would have added them. The parable was recorded and transmitted to us by the Evangelist Luke, and we are grateful to him. I am observing a degree of unrest in the audience. Father, what is this you're telling us here in the church? Is it ever advisable for us to succumb to the irrational demands of our immature children? Are we not to protect them from the dangers that lie in wait for them? Are we not to be strict and to set boundaries, prohibitions, and sanctions? Are going to allow the children to do anything they want to? Are we to satisfy all of their desires, without exceptions? Are we not sometimes obliged to restrain them?

What can I say to you? This evangelical parable today raises questions for me too, as I reread it. It draws me into another adventure, another way of thinking; it troubles me and in a way frightens me. Why did the father in the parable behave differently from the way we do? He did so simply because he is definitely not like us. He is God. He knows how to love far better than we do. He sees the past and the future as the present. He can see the depths. He knows the end of history. He does not judge superficially. He is unwilling to restrict the freedom of His creation. This is the freedom He gave us abundantly when He created us in the beginning. He is unable to diminish, remove, or bypass this human freedom and free will. This God-given gift of free will is inalienable.

The father in the parable was not encountering his son, then, for the first time. He knew him very well. He allowed him to open his heart. He himself had proven his love for him many times before. There was no need to repeat again and again the same things. The father had no desire to pressure his son, to force him, to crush him, to nail him down, to silence him, to insult him, to annihilate him. The father respected the son, loved him, was pained over him, and understood him quite well. He could not by any strategic means circumvent his freedom. Love has this superb nobility, this tremendous respect for the freedom of the other. Thus the father leaves the son with the choice he has made, even while knowing that the son will probably not succeed. It is difficult for someone to accept this, because it upsets our normal morality.

Do we listen to our children? Or do we only want to talk to them? And why, when we do in fact talk to them, must we talk to them loudly, imperatively, accusingly, harshly, threateningly, authoritatively, and violently? Our children are not only to be shouted at constantly; we must also listen to them a little at times. Do we in fact listen to them? Did we lovingly pay any attention to their struggles, their problems, their concerns, their fears, their doubts and questions and hesitations? Whatever it is we ask of our children, did we do it, or are we always doing it now? Have we ever listened to the observations of our children about us? Or have we, perhaps, never allowed them to make such observations about us? Could it be, perhaps, that our children do not listen to us because we do not listen to God? And if they do not listen and obey us, what do we do about it? Do we persist with the shouts, the curses, the threats, and the insults? Have we ever kneeled before the holy icons to beseech the Benevolent God to help us with the disobedience of our children? Have we humbled ourselves? Did we ever seek His help, His strength, His blessing, His enlightenment, and His consolation? Have we ever confessed and admitted our weakness before the Almighty God, who can do all things?

Sometimes, in our predicaments, we become excessive and thoughtless. The things we ourselves did not achieve, we expect our children to accomplish. Because we did not manage to become doctors, we expect our children to do so, without regard to whether or not they have the capacity to do so. We do not let them study what they like, but what will bring them more money. We even try to tell them what to wear, where to go, and which person they should marry. And yet God Himself, who rules over us, is not so overly authoritative with us.

Moreover, we behave like this not only with our children, but also with other adults around us and even with those we say we love. We always want to be the protagonists in the development of events, the center of conversations, the regulators of the life of others. We want to have the first and the last word; we want our will to be done and to always be the one who is right. We do not listen to what another person is saying, but are already thinking what we should say next to him. This is why the others seem to weary us so much. We want to exploit others, to use them as our peons or as a stepping-stone for our ascent. These are some of the reasons why today a rather stormy sea prevails in our society, which is just one way we may describe our highly disturbed interpersonal relationships.

This is why, my beloved friends, the father in the parable gave to his younger son directly the rightful portion of his estate when he asked for it. Certainly, the father had said many things to his son over the many years they were together. Many times and in many ways the father had indicated his love to his son. He did not think it proper to deprive him of his freedom, to block his departure, to convince him to stay willingly or not. He could not forcefully keep someone close against that person's will, as his slave, his servant, to be a dependent and at his constant beck and call. Love does not know this form of existence. The deprivation of freedom is sinful. The father allowed the beloved son to leave, to go far away, to fail in his adventure, that he might become prudent, come to his senses, correct himself, and truly repent.

God the Father is a free ruler, full of peace and love. This is how He wants His children to be also. We cannot comprehend the magnitude of His compassion, His love, and His freedom. God cannot be frightened by anything. Freedom requires very strong spiritual strength. We cannot or do not want to accept the other person as he is, as the one he really is. We like to intervene, to interfere directly and often rudely, in his life in order to correct him, to beautify him. But can we be so certain of our beautifying intentions for the other? Why is it that we are so excessively strict with others and so lenient with ourselves? Why do we not begin with ourselves? Why do we not exhaust our austere measures within ourselves? We are terribly easy-going with our criticism of others, while we are incredibly restrained when it comes to our own self-criticism. Why are we so diligently preoccupied with others but virtually not at all with ourselves? Why do we have so many justifications and excuses for ourselves but none for the others, our brothers, our neighbors?

We go around—and not only during Mardi Gras—with the masks of hypocrisy, pretension, alteration, and constant change. We are one thing and appear as another. At least the prodigal son appeared just as he was: ungrateful, unappreciative, impious, superficial, impudent, impertinent, daring, enthusiastic, and careless. He did not pretend to be God-fearing, somewhat unfortunate, and good like his brother. He presented his nakedness before his loving and grieving father. The father knew well the end result of his son's decisive actions. He did not prevent him; the son would not have obeyed anyway. At that time he was not listening to anyone. He had convinced himself that what he was doing was legal and therefore also ethical. He was not being unjust to anyone over anything. He was only fortifying his rights. He was not moved, at this time, by his father's love. He did not appreciate his father's silence, which was saying so much. The son did not suddenly recoil when he saw his father comply with his rebellion and give him directly whatever he demanded. Thus he took what was rightfully his and went far away, very far away, thinking that this way he could now move freely and be completely uncensored.

He imagined that in that far country he would not be followed by the loving glance of the father and the beautiful memories of the paternal home. He considered himself a victor—able to do now whatever he wanted undisturbed and without giving any account to anyone. He was deceiving himself. Soon enough he had squandered his money left and right by living a completely prodigal life. He considered self-control to be slavery, his home a prison, obedience lack of freedom, respect worthless, and cleanliness unnecessary. For the first time, he thought, he was living the joy of freedom and felt happy. But real happiness in sin can never exist. Without God, life is blurred, dull, dark, troubled, fearful, joyless, and difficult. The presumed happiness now turned into real misfortune.

A great famine came upon that far-away country where the prodigal son had gone. He was deprived of even the most basic things. He had nothing to eat, not even a morsel. With what money could he buy anything? He was a stranger, alone, poor, naked, hungry, thirsty, abandoned, penniless, homeless, dirty, sleepless, deprived of everything. This is how man ends up without God. In this miserable condition and with dragging feet, he went to be a swineherd and tried to fill his stomach with what the swine were eating. What a tragic irony this is, my brothers. He was eating the carob pods, which at first seem sweet, but then their harsh and bitter taste makes them inedible, as is the case with every sin.

In this terrible predicament—wounded, hurt, wronged, defeated, tired, degraded, embarrassed, and utterly exhausted—he began to recover. In the mire of his oppressive situation and with tears of regret, he remembered the home that he had abandoned, the love of the father, the wealth they had, the peace, the understanding, the prosperity, and the tranquility. He began to be nostalgic for his loving father, who did not chide him when he went away. This memory helped him greatly. On the contrary, if the father had threatened, cursed, or in some way disappointed him then, when he had asked to leave, it would have been impossible for the son to return now. Perhaps now we too can justify the father. He knew very well what he was doing. He did not see that he was being offended by his son, that his position as father was being refuted, that his authority was being insulted. Rather, he observed a troubled soul, that of his beloved son. He was not disregarding the son's future but rather was preparing for his return. Let us not be shortsighted. Let us not desire that all things go our way. Let us carefully consider the place of the other person. We will gain far more with leniency, patience, forgiveness, prayer, and hope.

The personal swamp of the prodigal son now became a springboard. His memory became a tender consolation. "How many of my father's hired servants have bread enough and to spare, and I perish with hunger! I will arise and go to my father, and will say to him, 'Father, I have sinned against heaven and before you, and I am no longer worthy to be called your son. Make me like one of your hired servants.'" These were not momentary words spoken only out of need. They came out of a profound pain: the pain of one who made himself a voluntary orphan, a lonely stranger who alienated himself into an isolated and loveless life. Surely his painful experience became the lesson that taught him. We are certainly not saying that we must first sin in order to hate sin. We must not and will not be led into sin in order that we can then repent. But if we do sin, we must not be disillusioned. Let us not allow ourselves to be led into the state of demonic hopelessness, into the painful state of remaining unrepentant. The young man in the parable learned the lesson well and took action.

He returned upon a familiar way. It is the way he had traversed quickly not long ago. With the same steady stride, he now returns, placing his hope upon the familiar love of his father. He has no doubts about this love. This love censures him, but it also draws him to return. The image he has of his father has not changed. He knows very well the father's great love. It is this that moves him and causes him to return. While the son is returning but is still at a considerable distance away, the father sees him. How did he see him? Well, he was always waiting for him. He was constantly expecting him. He was hoping for his return. He knew that his words had not gone to waste, even though he had not prevented the son from leaving in the first place. He was expecting him, looking out from the window and going to the outer gate for the reception. But how did he know that his son would be returning just then, when he was standing there and able to see him from a distance? But the father was always waiting for him, even from the moment the son left. This is something truly astonishing. The father was not offended, did not become angry, did not keep a grudge, and did not prepare a punishment or some revenge. He could not be without his son. It was impossible for him to reject his son. It did not matter that the son was somewhat lively, unruly, and disobedient; he was still his son. This was his particular cross, his temptation, and his struggle. He loved him; this prodigal was his son, and the father could not do otherwise.

Please note the magnificent scene. The father, who never stopped hoping, waiting, expecting, and observing the road, saw his son from a distance. He feels unimaginable joy. He does not think, "Ah, now that he has found difficulties and needs me, he is coming back. Wait and see what I will do to him now that he is again under my control. I will treat him most sternly to teach him that he cannot disobey me, overlook me, and embitter me. I will show him who I really am." The father in the parable, of course, does not at all think such base and dishonorable thoughts. In fact, and even though he is of considerable age, he does not remain waiting for his son in the parlor or even at the outer gate. He does not send his servants to bring and present him. He does not keep his place, his seat of honor and authority and power.

I told you, my dear friends, of an astonishing scene, with infinite beauty, emotion, and awe. The offended, insulted, and rejected elderly father saw his son, "had great compassion, and ran and fell on his neck and kissed him." Please forgive me for repeating myself. He did not stand there to count his possessions, to consider his perspective, and to establish the terms of his son's return. Nor did he wish to scrutinize the sincerity of his son's repentance or the intentions behind his return. He did not even wait to hear his son speak. What kind of father is this father? He did not merely go toward the son; he ran toward him. This has significant meaning. He did not merely greet him; he did not wait for him to bow, to kneel, to kiss his hand, to ask forgiveness. He did not even let him speak; there was no need to hear again the words he had rehearsed. The important thing was his presence. He seized him and embraced him. It was not a mere polite embrace but a full embrace, a tight hug. He did not merely kiss him, but "he kissed him again and again" (κατεφίλησε), covering him with kisses. This is truly an amazing scene, my friends. The culprit, the rebel, the impious, the prodigal, is embraced tightly and kissed many times by the loving father. This amazing father does not wait for the neutralization, the utter defeat, and the humiliation of his son's personality; he does not wait for the debasing and dissolution of his son. He also does not ask for justifications, promises, and heavy words. He does not even give him a chance to speak. He only embraces and kisses him with all of his fatherly love and paternal tenderness.

My dear friends, we must keep this scene and remember it well. It is very didactic and beneficial. This is the only and the permanent stance of our heavenly Father. Our God is not Zeus, who releases lightning rods against men. He is the God of love, compassion, mercy, goodness, and philanthropy. He is no rival who competes with us and waits at some corner to get even with us. He never takes revenge, never punishes, never keeps a grudge, and never gets angry. He patiently awaits the repentance of all, providing opportunities and never tiring of coming back for each one of us. He hopes for and prepares our return, always respecting the freedom that He Himself has given us. This exceptional image of the loving father provides great consolation and hope to all sinful persons.

The repentant prodigal son, in the embrace and kisses of his father, is crushed with contrition by the love of the father. "Look at who I am and how he behaves toward me! I have such a wonderful father, and look how badly I have behaved. Instead of punishing me, he embraces me; instead of imposing a penance, he smothers me with kisses. Your love, O father, has no boundaries. I am indeed unworthy of such good treatment. I am shaken to my very foundations by your behavior. Your love leaves me speechless; it completely disarms me. How I behaved, and how you now behave toward me! Why do you love me so much? I have not done anything to deserve such love from you. I cannot bear the magnitude of your love." In the father's embrace, the repentant son hears the beating of his father's heart. It beats for him. Within this indescribable warmth, he forgets the exile, the desertion, the loneliness, the cold, the filth, and the misery. He becomes calm and serene; he is transfigured, reborn, animated, and empowered.

On the other hand, it is as if the father is trying to tell the son, "Do not speak now. Do not destroy this most beautiful silence with frivolous vanities and unnecessary words. I know all things quite well. I was always with you. I followed you, and never abandoned you, even though you went away from me. I am not asking you for anything. I simply rejoice that you have returned. I thank you for returning to me. I am here and exist for you. For this reason I have created you: that we should always be together. We cannot live apart. Separation is bitter and a form of death. There is no need to express any justification. I was not vexed because you left; I am overjoyed because you returned. Now enjoy this happiness completely and never interrupt it, never allow it to be diminished. It is entirely in your hands, my son."

At some point the son is finally able to whisper these words, mingled with tears of true joy: "Father, I have sinned against heaven and in your sight, and am no longer worthy to be called your son." He spoke well; he knows what he is saying. He is not merely saying words about, nor making the gestures of, humility. He is now declaring before his father the truth that he actually feels. "How can I be your son, I who behaved with so much evil pride, while you are now acting with so much noble humility before me? I am really not worthy to be your son." The father does not interrupt him, does not correct him, and is not joyful over this confession. He heard him out very well and paid attention to what he said, but the father did not continue the thought and did not respond directly to the son's remarks. It is as if he did not hear and understand well what was said, while in fact he both heard and understood perfectly. The father turns and speaks to his servants as if to say, "Don't listen to him; he does not know what he is saying. Is it ever possible for my son not to be my son? Can I, the father who gave him life, not be at any point his father?" The attribute of being a father or a son is inalienable. So the father directs his servants to act accordingly: "Bring out the best robe and put it on him, and put a ring on his hand and sandals on his feet. And bring the fatted calf here and kill it, and let us eat and be merry; for this my son was dead and is alive again; he was lost and is found." This was done, and a very joyful celebration began. The Gospel says that such great joy takes place in heaven when a sinner repents.

In this entire bright festival, there was only one shadow. It came from the person of the older brother. According to the general consensus, he was a very good son. He was an obedient, honorable, quiet, and hard-working young man who never gave cause for trouble of any kind. Returning from the fields, where he had been working hard all day long, he noticed an unexpected change as he approached the house. Suddenly he saw the lights and heard the music and the dancing songs. Wondering what was going on, he called a servant to find out exactly what was happening. The servant then briefly told him, "Your brother, whom we all believed was lost, has returned, and your father decided to kill the fatted calf in his honor, for he has returned home safe and sound." What should have been the natural reaction upon hearing such news? To rejoice, to run and greet his brother who returned to their home. He did not do this. Why? He was so good and had never given cause to be criticized. Why now does he act this way? He did not simply become upset; he became very angry, very disturbed, and extremely agitated, because he did not expect anything like this. This unexpected return spoiled his plans. He himself had planned things quite differently. In regard to his prodigal brother, he felt superior. By comparison with his prodigal brother, he himself prevailed as the virtuous, innocent, and very good son. He could have and enjoy all the respect and love of his father. The return of the brother exasperated him. He did not even want to enter the house. He could not bear to see his brother. He went on to blame the father: "No, father, this is too much! We cannot be honoring the impious, the ungrateful, the embezzlers, the cunning, the indolent, and the foolish prodigals!"

When informed of the unbrotherly stance of older son, the father felt compelled to go out, to meet him, to speak sincerely to him and express his real intentions. The loving father understood fully his elder son's condition and began to speak to him, not in a scolding tone, but paternally, beseechingly, and lovingly. But the son did not want to listen and responded angrily and rudely: "Lo, these many years I have been serving you; I never transgressed your commandment at any time; and yet you never gave me a young goat, that I might make merry with my friends. But as soon as this son of yours came, who has devoured your livelihood with harlots, you killed the fatted calf for him."

The father listened to him carefully. He understood him very well. He saw in his son a change, a distortion in his character. He was not that older and mature son, the honorable, the sincere, the genuine, the solid, the serious, the unadorned, the unfeigned, the good and virtuous one. All these many years he had been pretending hypocritically; he went about masquerading, self-justified, self-sufficient, without love for honor, and most demanding. Unfortunately, he was not good, but played the role of being good. He could not bear it, and so his spiritual vacuum—his inner nakedness, ugliness, and agitation—was finally revealed. What a waste! So many lifelong efforts and labors were lost! The father does not try to come to terms with this petty rivalry. He is not disillusioned by the revelation of his son's actual inner world. He seems impervious to all the terrible things coming to light from his older son's soul. He does not cease loving him. He continues to plead with him and to invite him in: "My good son, you are always with me and I with you. Whatever is mine is also yours. I make no distinctions. I don't consider this yours and that mine. Don't be small-minded. Don't be misled by cleverly deceptive thoughts. Don't be jealous and envious and lose the opportunity to be joyful with us. Come and let us all rejoice together. This is a very significant day. This event gives reason for the whole world to rejoice. The person for whom we are rejoicing is not some unknown stranger. He is your only brother. He is my son. You are my son also. You are both my sons. Do not grieve me as he did. Please come into the house, I beg you, so we can all rejoice together. Your brother was dead and is alive again; he was lost and is found."

The parable seems to end rather abruptly. It does not tell us what happened to the elder son. Did his father convince him to go into the house and rejoice with the others? Perhaps he did not. The divine interpreters say no, it does not appear that he entered the house. If he had, this would have been noted for certain. The question is really serious. Let us examine it a little in the time we have left. At first glance it appears that the elder son is justified in his stance. He is accusing his father of being unjust to him. He believes that he is not receiving the proper recompense for the daily work he has been doing all along. And this stands in contrast to his prodigal brother, who receives an exceptional reception, an extraordinary honor, and a lavish banquet. But in honoring his repentant and returned son, the father is not being at all unjust to the elder son. The offered banquet is an expression of joy for the salvation of a soul. St. John Chrysostom reminds us that God sacrificed His Son on the Cross for the salvation of the human race.

It is a fact that in some areas the overabundant love of God for sinners seems to scandalize certain people. For some it is scandalous for God to have so much love for those repentant sinners. The righteous and divine justice of God is different from the human justice of men. It is particularly remarkable that clergy and spiritual people who work in the Church for years can hide an inner sense of some sort of superiority over against those who are not in the Church. It is possible for a hidden and latent pharisaic spirit to breed and incubate for a long time: "We are not like those other people; we are different and on a somewhat higher plane than they, and because of this status, sooner or later we must be recognized and honored." We forget that sinners can actually repent and be saved, whereas we remain in our unhealthy, narcissistic, and presumed spirituality, feeling misunderstood and free to easily judge everybody else. It so happens that the followers of the elder son in the parable have far more rights before God; they are deserving of a better position and a better reward. They think highly of themselves and take an unacceptable, demanding stance before God. Sometimes they even have a rather repulsive hardness, impatience, absoluteness, self-confidence, and a controlling authoritarianism.

They forget, unfortunately, that repentance and humility are superior to those good works, which in themselves do not justify us, as St. Mark the Ascetic reminds us. St. Cyril of Alexandria also emphasizes that the salvation of man is a gift from God to man, and is not the result of a few or of many good works. According to the well-spoken observation of Metropolitan Joel of Edessa, in the mind of many ethicists the thief, the prostitute, the publican, the prodigal, and many other persons like them should not have been saved. But God is an ocean of love and wants to save all of mankind. Only the obstinate, those who do not repent, will not be saved. St. Isaac the Syrian says characteristically that God may indeed be called just, but He is far more benevolent and good. From us He asks that we offer to Him a clean heart.

The elder son in the parable proved to be more immature spiritually than the younger son. The younger one, with his true repentance, was able to correct and clear away all of his mistakes. The elder son, with his obstinate refusal to repent, lost even the good things he had gained through years of work and self-control, and in the end did not enter into the joy of the feast. The hardness of his presumed virtue left him without brotherly love, and he was thus self-condemned. Our God—the God of love, benevolence, and goodness—loves us to the superlative degree and is constantly providing opportunities for us to repent. He especially loves those who are direct and sincere and unfeigned in their personality. As the blessed elder Paisios the Haghiorite has said, "One profound sigh from the heart and a heartfelt 'Lord have mercy' have much more weight than a bucket of sentimental tears and wearisome pietistic trivialities."

God loves very much those who love him and who also love those other neighbors unsparingly, uncompromisingly, and without expecting something in exchange. He particularly loves the prayers we offer for others—the poor, the wronged, the slandered, the sick, the lonely, the prodigal, and the hypocritical. Fr. Eusebius Vittes, who recently fell asleep in the Lord, speaks very beautifully and prayerfully as he invites us to confess sincerely before the Lord, who sees all, even the depths of our heart: "Our soul serves the senses; it is enslaved to the passions, bound to pride, wounded by hypersensitivity, egotistical beyond imagination, loose and uncommitted beyond precedent, suspicious without reason, indifferent and negligent, sluggish to the point of paralysis, tightly bound to the world, short on faith at times of temptation, extremely poor in virtues, and with insignificant spiritual progress."

Before we conclude this presentation, my dear friends, we must understand something and make a decision. The present parable is replete with personal messages. We need not repeat them. Let us reach out and take hold of something and keep it well. In the end, both sons proved to be prodigals. Each one was a prodigal in his own way. The younger son repented practically and sincerely. The elder son dropped his mask, but it seems that he could not bear his nakedness and did not repent. He did not enter into the Eucharistic banquet; he had learned to live with the false mask. The two brothers are our brothers. We are all, my brothers, some more and some less, fellow sufferers, fellow craftsmen, and wearing masks. We always have the same Father, who unreservedly respects our freedom and is expecting us—in order that He may embrace us and kiss us, forgive us, put a new garment on us, offer us a banquet, and love us as before.

The repentant prodigal accompanies us and motivates us to follow the beautiful way of sweet return. He is our fellow traveler and fellow supporter; he is a companion and a helper in our efforts, our restorations, our aspirations, our anxieties, our struggles, our tears, our petitions, and our setbacks. Life in the land of exile became a torment in the end. He became weary; he experienced many difficulties, worries, and severe buffetings that in the end left him completely disillusioned. He expected one thing, and what he found was quite another. He sought pleasure and found pain. He sought freedom and tasted bitter slavery. Without consolation, without strength, powerless, timid, small, helpless, deceived, and disheartened, how did he manage to be raised up? He was saved by the memory of the innocent years of his youth, the peace of the paternal home, the magnanimous heart of his most-compassionate father. His father never abandoned him. The father never behaved toward the son as the son behaved toward him. The son's thought that he could once again indeed be with the father dispelled all his fears, hesitation, postponement, and desire to move from place to place. The elder Porphyrios Kausokalyvites used to say, "Do to me, O Christ, whatever You want, but let me always be near You!" The tribulations made the prodigal strong. He returned to the father that he might become a mere servant, and the father took him into his heart and showered him with loving kisses. When we give a little to God, He in turn gives us much, much more. But it is imperative that we take that first step, to indicate that we do want Him to be the Lord of our life, the delight of our heart.

The spiritual life is not difficult, unachievable, strange, complex, or individualistic; it does not reject others and certainly is not a means to gain personal comfort and ease. The elder son had an entirely false understanding of the spiritual life. He thought that because he never left the home, always worked hard, did not spend the nights with his friends eating and drinking and dancing, he was also a saintly person. He did not become a prodigal, but it seems that somewhere deep inside himself he yearned for it. This is why he was so hard with his younger brother. Even the desire to sin is sinful. The pollution of the sinners is also inadmissible. The elder son had his share of false and unhealthy elements in his unorthodox spirituality. With his hard and unyielding stance, he hurt both his brother and his father; he dishonored, mocked, humiliated, wronged, and disregarded them. He had "a zeal without knowledge" that made him unusually fussy, peculiar, curiously prying, rude, and ill fated.

Whoever we are, whatever we are, wherever we have come to be, even at the very edge of the abyss, we must never let go of the moving image of the prodigal son's reception into the embrace of the father, who hugs him tightly and showers him with kisses. Let our final fall be into the arms of our most-compassionate heavenly Father, so that He may embrace and kiss us, and open to us the gates of His all-blessed and endless kingdom according to His great mercy and most-compassionate love. Amen.

www.ingramcontent.com/pod-product-compliance
Lightning Source LLC
LaVergne TN
LVHW011426080426
835512LV00005B/288